AFRICAN WORLD HISTORIES

Sovereignty and Struggle
Africa and Africans in the Era of the Cold War 1945–1994

AFRICAN WORLD HISTORIES

Series Editor:
Trevor R. Getz, San Francisco State University

African World Histories is a series of retellings of some of the most commonly discussed episodes of the African and global past from the perspectives of Africans who lived through them. Accessible yet scholarly, *African World Histories* gives students insights into African experiences and perspectives concerning many of the events and trends that are commonly discussed in the history classroom.

Titles in the Series

Published
Cosmopolitan Africa, 1700–1875
Trevor R. Getz, San Francisco State University

Colonial Africa, 1884–1994
Dennis Laumann, University of Memphis

Transatlantic Africa, 1440–1800
Kwasi Konadu, City University of New York, and
Trevor R. Getz, San Francisco State University

Africanizing Democracies, 1980–Present
Alicia Decker, Penn State University, and Andrea Arrington,
University of Arkansas

*Sovereignty and Struggle: Africa and Africans in the Era
of the Cold War, 1945–1994*
Jonathan T. Reynolds, Northern Kentucky University

Forthcoming
Bantu Africa
Christine Saidi, Kutztown University; Catherine Symone
Fourshay, Susquehanna University; Rhonda M. Gonzalez,
University of Texas at San Antonio

AFRICAN WORLD HISTORIES

Sovereignty and Struggle

Africa and Africans in the Era of the Cold War

1945–1994

Jonathan T. Reynolds

Northern Kentucky University

New York Oxford
OXFORD UNIVERSITY PRESS

Oxford University Press is a department of the University of Oxford.
It furthers the University's objective of excellence in research,
scholarship, and education by publishing worldwide.

Oxford   New York
Auckland   Cape Town   Dar es Salaam   Hong Kong   Karachi
Kuala Lumpur   Madrid   Melbourne   Mexico City   Nairobi
New Delhi   Shanghai   Taipei   Toronto

With offices in
Argentina   Austria   Brazil   Chile   Czech Republic   France   Greece
Guatemala   Hungary   Italy   Japan   Poland   Portugal   Singapore
South Korea   Switzerland   Thailand   Turkey   Ukraine   Vietnam

For titles covered by Section 112 of the US Higher Education
Opportunity Act, please visit www.oup.com/us/he for the
latest information about pricing and alternate formats.

Published by Oxford University Press
198 Madison Avenue, New York, New York 10016
http://www.oup.com

Library of Congress Cataloging-in-Publication Data
Reynolds, Jonathan T., author.
  Sovereignty and struggle : Africa and Africans in the era of the
Cold War, 1945–1994 / Jonathan T. Reynolds, Northern Kentucky University
    pages cm. -- (African world histories)
  ISBN 978-0-19-991512-5
  1. Africa--Politics and government--1960- 2. Africa--Politics and government--
1945–1960. 3. Cold War--Political aspects--Africa. 4. Decolonization--Africa--
History. I. Saunders, Christopher C., author. II. Title. III. Series: African world
histories.
  DT30.5.R495 2014
  960.32--dc23
                                                                   2014025577
Printing number: 9 8 7 6 5 4 3 2

Printed in the United States of America
on acid-free paper

Dedication

To my siblings Glenn, Katy, and Brad. With love.

CONTENTS

Maps and Figures

MAPS

FIGURES

Acknowledgments

Thanks to Trevor Getz and Charles Cavaliere for inviting me to do this book and letting it be fun. Special thanks to my dear wife, Dr. Ngozi Victoria Uti, and our children William and Ojie for their patience and support. A hat tip to my very cool department chair, William Landon. A shout-out goes to my "Africa Since WORLD WAR II" students who used an early draft of this text, with special nods to James McManus, Christopher Crigler, and Matthew Wallin. Thanks also to Kevin Kuhn, who provided me with much useful information about Ghana Airways. My appreciation goes to colleagues Eric Jackson, Meredith Smith, Jacob Tropp, and Lisa Lindsay for reading and offering insights on early draft chapters. Thanks to uber-librarian David Atkins. *Shokran* to Katya Belhabib for schooling me on *Rai*. Cool guys Dr. Jeremy Rich and Chap Godbey did a great job of introducing me to some killer African bands and artists. I also wish to thank the following reviewers who provided helpful advice: Saheed Aderinto, Western Carolina University; Matthew M. Heaton, Virginia Tech; Nate Plageman, Wake Forest University; George White, Jr., York College, CUNY; Kenneth Wilburn, East Carolina University. Thanks also to my longtime friend and colleague Erik Gilbert, whose keen insights and wit inform my work even when we aren't collaborating. Any errors are of course my own. Much of the research on which this volume is based was undertaken with the support of West African Research Association and Northern Kentucky University fellowships in 2000.

About the Author

As an undergraduate at the University of Tennessee, Jonathan T. Reynolds majored in Honors History, Anthropology, and Ancient Mediterranean Civilizations. Finishing his dissertation on Islam and decolonization in Northern Nigeria, at Boston University in 1995, he soon found himself teaching African history, African American history, Middle Eastern history, world history, food history, and historical methodology, first at Livingstone College and later at Northern Kentucky University. Along the way he coauthored *Africa in World History* and *Trading Tastes* with Erik Gilbert. Their world history textbook, *World in Motion: A Dynamic History of Humankind*, will soon be released. At Livingstone he received the Aggrey Teacher of the Year Award. At Northern Kentucky University he received the Outstanding Junior Faculty, Excellence in Sustained Research, the Alumni Association Strongest Influence, and the Milburn Outstanding Professor awards. He has served on the Executive Board of the World History Association and is an associate editor for *World History Connected.* When not teaching, writing, cooking, or larking about with his kids, he can be found playing music around the Cincinnati area with his cool band mate Blake Taylor in the semi-acoustic duo 46 Long.

Series Introduction

African World Histories is a new approach to teaching and learning for African history and African studies courses. Its main innovation is to approach African and global experiences from the perspectives of the Africans who lived through them. By integrating accounts and representations produced or informed by Africans with accessible scholarly interpretations in both local and global frameworks, *African World Histories* gives students insight into Africans' understandings and experiences of such episodes as the Atlantic slave trade, the growth of intercontinental commerce and the industrial revolution, colonialism, and the Cold War. The authors in this series do this by looking at culture, politics, social organization, daily life, and economics in an integrated format using the most recent studies as well as primary source materials. Unlike those of many textbooks and series, the authors of *African World History* actively take positions on major issues like the centrality of violence in the colonial experience, the cosmopolitan nature of pre-colonial African societies, and the importance of democratization in Africa today. Underlying this approach is the belief that students can succeed when presented with relatively brief, jargon-free interpretations of African societies that integrate Africans' perspectives with critical interpretations and that balance intellectual rigor with broad accessibility.

This series is designed for use both in world history and African history/studies classrooms. As an African history/studies teaching tool it combines continent-wide narratives with emphases on specific, localized, and thematic stories that help demonstrate wider trends. As an auxiliary text for the world history classroom, the volumes in this series can help to illuminate important episodes in the global past from the perspectives of Africans, adding complexity and depth as well as facilitating intellectual growth for students. Thus it will help world history students understand not only that the human past was "transnational" and shared, but also how it was understood differently by different groups and individuals.

The volume you hold in your hands, *Sovereignty and Struggle*, is a particularly rich interpretation of the African past. The author has done an incredible job of bringing together cultural sources like music and popular art to tell the story of a continent learning to be free once again and of people striving to shape their own modernities and contributions in a complex world.

African World Histories is the product of a grand collaboration. The authors include scholars from around the world and across Africa. Each volume was reviewed by multiple professionals in African history and related fields. The excellent team of editors at Oxford University Press, led by Charles Cavaliere, put a great deal of effort into commissioning, reviewing, and bringing these volumes to publication. Finally, we all stand on the shoulders of giants in the field like A. Adu Boahen, Chiekh Anta Diop, Joseph Ki-Zerbo, Jan Vansina, Roland Oliver, and many others.

—**TREVOR R. GETZ, SERIES EDITOR**

Introduction

It was the winter of 2010, and I was a busy man. I had classes to teach, a family to raise, and books and articles to write. And then I got an email from Trevor Getz. He wanted me to write a book on Africa from about 1945 to 1994 for an Oxford University Press series he was editing. Now, in the world of academia, that's a pretty generous offer. But, as I said, I was busy.

I politely turned him down.

He persisted. Trevor Getz is a very persistent guy.

In the end we reached an accommodation. Years ago I had collected some really cool material relating to Ghana during the 1950s and 1960s. A lot of it had to do with cars, airplanes, and the flight attendants known as "air girls." This material made me very happy, but I had never quite figured out how to put it to use. More recently I had begun to collect large quantities of African rock, funk, and soul music from the late 1960s and 1970s. So I told him I would do the book if I got to write about air girls and rock and roll. I'm pretty sure that somewhere in there I made him promise that he would let me make the book "funky," too. In return I assured him that I would discuss more conventional political, economic, and cultural topics along the way. He said this sounded like a cunning plan.

Sovereignty and Struggle: Africa and Africans in the Era of the Cold War is the result of that accommodation. The title itself seeks to grapple with the complexity of African and world history in the decades following World War II. At the end of the war, the world was a very different place than it had been just a few years before. The once-mighty colonial powers of Western Europe were in economic, political, and cultural disarray. New superpowers increasingly dominated global politics. Around the world, populations who had been denied the right to make choices as individuals and as communities were demanding and gradually receiving the right to do so. That's where the *Sovereignty* part of the title comes from. For example, a country that gets to set its own laws and policies is considered sovereign. Similarly, people exercise personal sovereignty when they choose where and how they want to live. There are lots of other words that we use to denote or describe the process of gaining sovereignty and being sovereign. These include such terms as decolonization, liberation, revolution, independence, and freedom. Most people think sovereignty is a good thing, though in practice many individuals and groups are not comfortable with everybody having complete sovereignty. Thus, much of the story told in this book is about the process of how Africans went about getting and using sovereignty in the years following 1945.

The *Struggle* part comes from the fact that neither getting sovereignty nor taking advantage of sovereignty is necessarily easy. First, the process of decolonization required that African populations force reluctant colonial states to yield power over their lives. Sometimes this end was achieved through relatively peaceful processes such as demonstrations, strikes, and negotiations. In others, violence, ranging from riots, to sabotage, to wars of liberation, was required for gaining independence. But the struggle did not end with the creation of new nations. Sovereignty is a slippery thing. Very few nations or individuals get to do whatever they want whenever they want. This was all the more true for newly independent states, for which choices were often limited by economic and political realities. As such, another component of the struggle was for newly independent states and peoples to make the sovereignty that independence tantalizingly offered a reality. Doing so, however, meant navigating and implementing a host of political, economic, and cultural choices. These ranged from matters as simple as "should we build a new brewery?" to somewhat more complex topics such as "should we create a Pan African Union?" Notably, the popular consensus is that African states did a poor job of making such choices in the first decades after independence, at least as judged by the generally poor track record of improving the quality of life of most African populations during that period. Although not denying that most African states certainly could have done better, this book seeks to show that the choices made by African states were difficult ones, that African leaders were not alone in making the choices they did, and that these choices were informed not only by the pursuit of national development, but also by survival in a very complex and often dangerous world.

And this is what brings us to the *Era of the Cold War* part. The subtitle of this text could easily have been "Africa from 1945 to 1994." However, I chose to identify this period thematically for the simple fact that I believe the global context of the Cold War to have played a crucial part in much of what happened during the time period in question. This doesn't necessarily mean that all Africans spent their days fretting over global politics or fearing nuclear annihilation, but neither does it mean that many Africans didn't do either on a fairly regular basis. Certainly on the national and regional levels, Cold War politics often played a dramatic and often destructive role in influencing the course of African events. As I have written elsewhere, "Gaining independence during the Cold War was like getting your driver's license in the middle of a demolition derby."[1] Thus it is crucial for readers to realize that what is often considered to have been a largely ideological conflict in the United States or Soviet Union was, in many other parts of the world, a very real and all too often deadly conflict with significant political, economic, and even cultural impacts on people's day-to-day lives.

To this end, *Sovereignty and Struggle* approaches its subject matter in five chapters. The first three are relatively straightforward thematic approaches dealing with the politics of early liberation struggles, economics, and global Cold War complexities. The goal of these chapters is to provide readers with insight into the motivations and aspirations of Africans from around the continent during the period in question. The last two chapters focus on what is often called "popular culture" and are, I hope, a bit more funky. Chapter 4 deals with music, nation building, and identity. Chapter 5 focuses on popular representations of mobility, modernity, and sovereignty in Ghana during the 1950s and 1960s. In preparing these chapters, I sought to balance a broad knowledge of the continent with carefully chosen local case studies. With the goal of providing a degree of narrative coherence to the text, I have made a point of presenting at least some material relating to Ghana in each chapter. Ghana was chosen in part because of its role in not only blazing a trail to decolonization, nonalignment, and Pan-Africanism that many other African states followed, but also because it was an example of African political and economic decline in the 1960s and 1970s and a model of African rebirth in the 1990s and afterward. And did I mention I also had lots of really cool Ghanaian material that I had collected and not found a suitable historical home for? Yes, yes I did.

In so approaching the history of Africa and the world during this crucial period of recent history, I hope that this short text will

---

[1] Gilbert and Reynolds, p. 385.

highlight the complexity of the struggles undertaken, the choices made, the chances taken, the victories won, the failures suffered, and the lives led. More so, I encourage you, the reader, to think about how the stories told in these chapters highlight the degree to which all our lives on this planet have been, and continue to be, connected and shared.

JONATHAN T. REYNOLDS
Northern Kentucky University
April, 2014

REFERENCE

Gilbert, Erik and Jonathan T. Reynolds. *Africa in World History: From Prehistory to the Present* (Upper Saddle River, New Jersey: Pearson, 2011).

A World Set Free?
African Decolonization
in the Era of Liberation

The world in 1900 was in many ways a very different place than the one we live in today. In the latter half of the nineteenth century, European armies undertook massive multidecade campaigns that brought much of Africa, Southeast Asia, and other world regions under colonial control. At the beginning of the twentieth century, European powers were consolidating a wave of colonial conquests that had given them political, economic, and, to a certain degree, cultural influence over a huge swath of the world. By 1918, with the collapse of the Ottoman Empire, much of what we call the Middle East would also be added to this colonial dominion. Meanwhile, in the Americas, the United States was flexing its own growing power in Central America, the Caribbean, and Latin America. Such developments guaranteed the flow of cheap commodities to feed the growing demand for industrial production and consumption in industrialized Europe and North America. One of the outcomes of this rather unexpected course of global events was that power was concentrated in the hands of a tiny percentage of the world's population. More specifically, power was concentrated in the hands of a few wealthy men who happened to be what we call "white." Although colonialism certainly did not wrest all authority and influence from the hands of nonwhite peoples and women, it did have the effect of placing white men at the pinnacles of the pyramids of power that regulated how the world worked at this particular point in time. As such, the early twentieth century was a good time to be a white male—especially one who was wealthy, educated, or both. This was in no small part because the expansion of European power conferred on white males a greater degree of *sovereignty* than it apportioned to nonwhite men and women of all colors. At its most basic level, sovereignty is the right to make choices—and white men not only got to make more choices regarding their own lives, but many of them got to make choices for those for whom sovereignty was restricted or denied. More so, a host of philosophical, theological, and biological arguments were used to justify a state of this state of affairs so as to present this gendered and racial hegemony as "natural."

But every high point is also a turning point. Perhaps one of the most significant themes of the twentieth century is that it saw a dramatic expansion in the distribution of sovereignty. Beginning with the advent of women's suffrage in Europe and America, and proceeding with calls for greater rights among nonwhite populations both in the industrialized and colonized worlds, the twentieth century increasingly saw the dismantling of institutionalized white male privilege and the extension of sovereignty to both individuals and regions who had been denied even the most basic of choices about how their affairs and lives were to be led. By the end of the twentieth century, the idea that white men were "naturally" superior to women and nonwhite men had gone from being an underpinning assumption of the global power structure to a fringe position largely associated with extremism and bigotry. In examining this transformation, this chapter focuses on what is often called the period of independence in Africa, but it does so by placing the end of colonial rule and the quest of African sovereignty in the context of struggles for liberation that were taking place around the world. Such an approach will help us to better understand the global context of African decolonization, as well as how African liberation helps us to better understand the meaning and significance of what was happening elsewhere in the world during the tumultuous period of the mid-twentieth century. In so doing, this chapter first examines the global context of the postwar era. Next comes an overview of the different routes to decolonization taken in different parts of Africa. Also investigated is the attention given by some Africans to other liberation movements elsewhere in the world. Finally, this chapter undertakes an examination of the movement for and debate over Pan-Africanism in the early independence era. In so doing, this chapter focuses mainly on events up to and including the 1960s.

A NEW WORLD AT MIDCENTURY? AFRICA AND THE WORLD AFTER WORLD WAR II

Although many histories focus on the conflict in Europe and the Pacific during World War II, it is important to remember that the war encompassed much of the world. Indeed, the brutal Italian invasion of Ethiopia in October of 1935 was one of the first incidences of fascist aggression. One of the war's major campaigns took place in North Africa in 1942 and 1943. More so, hundreds of thousands of African troops served in regions ranging from Southeast Asia to Europe. Such service, as in World War I before, helped create a class of cosmopolitan ex-servicemen who had seen the world and forged connections with far-flung populations brought together by imperial militaries. Even those who did not serve abroad felt the impact of the war as demands for production of food and raw materials to feed industrial war machines increased. These demands, combined with higher taxes and wartime rationing of imported goods, also stressed populations in Africa—sometimes to the point of famine and rebellion.

The very nature of World War II as a conflict pitting democratic and communist allies against fascist foes was also significant. The allied powers, including the British, Free French, United States, and Soviet Union, each stressed the nature of the war as a struggle of freedom against oppression and evil. In turn, Germany, Italy, and Japan sought to define the war as an effort to overthrow communism and imperialism. Colonized populations in Africa and elsewhere were more than aware of the irony of this situation. Many Africans, especially among the growing political and economic elite, recognized the racism and brutality of fascism. Indeed, British wartime propaganda often stressed fascist racism, quoting directly from *Mein Kampf* and citing the invasion of Ethiopia to highlight German and Italian contempt for black Africans. Yet these populations could hardly fail to note that the colonialism imposed by allied powers such as Britain and France was different at best in degree, but certainly not in kind, from fascist oppression. African soldiers serving in the war recognized the hypocrisy of fighting for freedom in much the same way as did African American soldiers from the segregated United States. For Africans in French colonies the meaning of the war was particularly complex, as competing French administrations first resisted, then allied to, and then broke with the axis powers.

The eventual defeat of fascism at the end of World War II did little to settle matters in Africa. Like World War I, the conflict did much to bring greater awareness of European failings to African populations. African servicemen brought back tales of European brutality, suffering, and destruction—stories that reflected the reality of a Europe ravaged and bankrupted by conflict of epic scale. The rapid progress of India and Middle Eastern states toward independence and the challenge to continued colonial presence in Indochina highlighted the growing ability of colonized peoples to demand and assert their sovereignty. Similarly, the rise of the United States and the Soviet Union highlighted the eclipse of European power not only because of these new superpowers' military and economic might, but also because they shared a common anticolonial rhetoric despite their own competition for imperial influence. Indeed, as we will see in this chapter and others, it was the irony, hypocrisy, and complexity of the Cold War that would in so many ways fuel and complicate Africa's quest for political and economic independence.

But the demands for greater sovereignty in the postwar world were not simply made by colonized peoples against colonizers. They grew in volume among certain populations within the industrialized countries themselves. In the United States, for example, African Americans, Native Americans, women, and LGBT (Lesbian, Gay, Bisexual, and Transgender) populations increasingly organized and clamored for not just suffrage, but for equal legal protection, access to education, freedom of movement, and rights to person. In so doing, they too were inspired by the way the battle against fascism had highlighted the uneven distribution of sovereignty even in the world's democracies. And here is an excellent case of revolution begetting revolution. In this case, the revolutions in transportation and communications technology increasingly brought news of struggles for sovereignty in one part world to another. Thus the struggles of the colonized in Africa and Asia were both informed by and resonated with the struggles of minorities and women in the industrialized world. Therefore, in many respects, these seemingly diverse movements were related and mutually reinforcing. An age of liberation was taking shape.

ROUTES TO DECOLONIZATION IN AFRICA

Demands for greater sovereignty and even decolonization were certainly not new to the postwar era. African leaders and populations had at times protested, demanded, and even fought for an end to colonial domination during the early twentieth century. The role of African American and West Indian activists such as W.E.B. DuBois and Marcus Garvey in encouraging these calls for liberation is also significant. These demands rapidly grew in volume and force in the decade following World War II (see Map 1.1). More so, it is important to recognize that these demands made a great deal of sense. During both the Great Depression

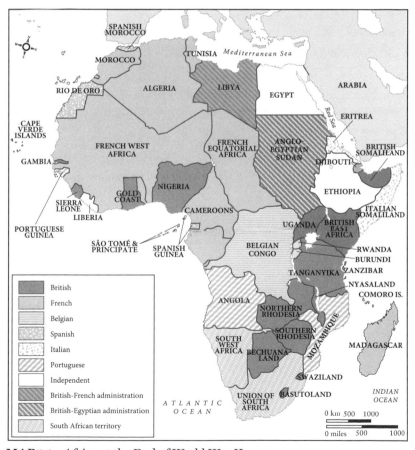

MAP 1.1 Africa at the End of World War II

and World War II, most African colonies had to be economically self-sufficient and fund their own "development." Just as World War II highlighted the immorality of colonial exploitation, the conflict also reinforced Africa's economic potential. African production, in particular, had helped maintain the allied war effort. It was apparent to many Africans that European powers had profited far more from colonialism than had Africans. Would not an end to colonial exploitation then lead to rapid economic growth? Further, the pressure placed on Africans to defend colonial powers during European conflicts was resented by many African elites. Witness the following excerpt from a speech delivered by the Nigerian nationalist Nnamdi Azikiwe in 1949:

> When the Allied Powers sounded the tocsin for World War I, Africa played a leading role not only as a supplier of men, materials, and money, but as a theatre of war in which German Colonialism in the Cameroons, in East Africa, and in South West Africa was destroyed. Again, when the Allied Nations beat the tom-tom for World War II, the African continent was used by military strategists in order to destroy the Fascist aims of Germany, Italy, and Vichy France. It is very significant that in the last two world wars, African peoples were inveigled into participating in the destruction of their fellow human beings on the grounds that Kaiserism and Hitlerism must be destroyed in order that the world should be made safe for democracy—a political theory which seems to be an exclusive property of the good peoples of Europe and America, whose rulers appear to find war a profitable mission and enterprise.[1]

The fact that Azikiwe's speech was given in London further highlights the significance of the increased mobility of colonized populations in the postwar era.

The smoothness of the routes to decolonization, as well as their length, however, was to vary significantly in different regions of the continent, however. For the sake of clarity, this section examines the path to decolonization in North Africa, British Africa, French Africa, and Belgian Africa separately. The path to decolonization in Portuguese Africa and Anglophone South Africa will be left largely to Chapter 3, because of both the somewhat later date of the movement to independence in these regions and the growing influence of Cold War rivalries. Do note, however, that these divisions are in many ways artificial (as are all historical categories of analysis) and that developments and ideas in each setting were connected and mutually influential.

---

[1] Azikiwe, pp. 61–62.

Decolonization in North Africa

For a number of different reasons, the states of the Middle East and North Africa proceeded to independence somewhat more swiftly than did those of the rest of the continent. Some of these reasons had to do with European racial attitudes, and others had to do with the region's economic and political status.

It was Egypt, with its multimillennium history of state-level governance, that led the push for independence in the region. Egypt had gained nominal independence from Britain in 1922, but many elements in Egypt, particularly those organized in the Arab Socialist Party, resented continued British control of the Suez Canal and the presence of large numbers of British troops. Tensions also resulted from Egyptian claims to sovereignty over the region of the Sudan to the south. Following World War II, the Egyptian government, under the leadership of King Farouk, pushed for the withdrawal of British troops and greater autonomy, but popular discontent was growing both as a response to poor economic and social progress and as a result of the poor performance of Egyptian troops in the 1948 war with the new state of Israel. In 1952, a group of young military officers calling themselves the Free Officers Movement launched a coup that overthrew Farouk and in 1953 established a new constitution transforming Egypt into a Republic. Western powers, particularly the British and the United States, were concerned by the Free Officers' calls for nonalignment in the Cold War and Pan-Arab nationalism. Egypt's expanded economic and diplomatic connections with the Soviet Union and recognition of China, for example, eventually led to the withdrawal of US funding for the planned dam of the Nile River at Aswan.

In 1956, tensions between Egypt and Britain came to a head when Egypt, under its new president, Gamal Abdel Nasser, declared the nationalization of the Suez Canal. Seeing this as an unacceptable blow to British economic and strategic interests, the British cooperated with France and Israel to stage a crisis in the region and then sent in troops to secure the Suez. In the ensuing hostilities, Egypt's military fought tenaciously despite heavy losses and succeeded in blocking the canal, which brought substantial economic pressure to bear in Europe and across the Atlantic. Notably, the Suez Crisis (as it came to be known) was in the end largely resolved when the United States and the Soviet Union together demanded an end to the British and French efforts to reclaim the canal. Thus Egypt's assertion of full sovereignty over the canal zone was not only a major step in the country's drive for independence, but also a major turning point in the decline of colonial influence and a major event in the Cold War.

Farther west in North Africa, Algeria was another crucial locus in the struggle for decolonization. Invaded by the French in 1830, Algeria had become a destination for French immigrants who were attracted to the excellent farmlands and cosmopolitan cities along the region's Mediterranean coast. Leveraging their French status, these settlers, also known as *colons* (colonizers) or *pied noir* (black feet), were able to take control of the region's finest lands and exercise a degree of economic and political autonomy denied to native Algerians. Beginning in 1848, the French began to administer northern Algeria not as a colony, but as an overseas province of France. By the mid-twentieth century more than one million ethnic French lived in Algeria—some recent arrivals, but others who had by this time lived in Algeria for two or three generations. A small number of Algerians who had assimilated to French culture had also been granted citizenship. The vast majority of the Algerian population, however, had never embraced either union with France or the presence of French settlers. On November 1, 1954, the *Front de libération nationale* (National Liberation Front or FLN) launched a campaign of armed resistance that first targeted government buildings and infrastructure.

Inspired by the successes of the Vietnamese against the French in Indochina and aided by Egypt and also by neighboring Morocco and Tunisia (which gained independence from France in 1956), the FLN stepped up its campaign. A crucial step was when the FLN chose to target French civilians and Algerian "collaborators"—killing 123, including women and children, at the Phillipville Massacre in 1955. Violence quickly escalated as the French military and *pied noir* vigilante groups launched reprisals known as *ratissages* (rat hunts) against Algerian populations, resulting in the deaths of thousands. By 1957 the conflict had attracted international attention and was dubbed the "Battle of Algiers" as conflict came to be centered in the capital city. The FLN bombings and shootings numbered in the hundreds per month, and a national strike by Algerians shut the region's economy down. The French responded with martial law and authorized the use of any methods necessary to break the rebellion—including the use of mass incarceration, torture, and the widespread killing of civilians. Press coverage of the atrocities committed by both sides shocked the world. Although the French were able to declare victory in the "Battle" by 1958 and shatter much of the FLN's infrastructure, the damage to France's international reputation was devastating.

When the French government attempted to normalize the administration of the region in 1958, *pied noir* mobs seized control of the Algerian administration, and French military extremists (known as "ultras") in Algeria made thinly veiled threats that they would launch a coup against the French government in Paris unless Charles de Gaulle were returned to power—bringing down the French Fourth Republic and bringing de Gaulle out of retirement. But the hopes that the ultras and *colons* placed in de Gaulle were misguided. He attempted to purge the ultras from the French military and launched a campaign to cultivate Algerian moderates that included extending the franchise to all Algerian men and women and investing in education and infrastructure. In 1959 de Gaulle proposed a referendum to allow Algerians to choose the future of their relationship with France. Both the FLN and French settler extremists responded by launching renewed attacks on civilian populations. By 1960, former ultra elements had joined with settler groups to form the *Organisation de l'armée secrète* (Secret Army Organization or OAS), which launched attacks not only on Algerians, but also on the French administration and military in Algeria. They also launched a brief insurrection in Algiers and other cities in January of 1960. When the referendum was held in January 1961 it revealed overwhelming support for Algerian independence both in Algeria and France, and de Gaulle moved to begin secret negotiations with the FLN for independence. In response, on April 21, 1961, a group of dissident French military officers, including several retired generals, launched a coup attempt first in Algeria but with plans to overthrow the de Gaulle government as well. Espousing both nationalist and anticommunist rhetoric, the coup plotters sought to halt any move toward Algerian independence. Stymied by a televised call for loyalty by de Gaulle, the coup attempt did much to finally delegitimize the efforts to keep Algeria as a part of France.

Following the failed coup, de Gaulle renewed the negotiations with the FLN, and on July 3, 1962, Algeria was declared an independent state. Nearly a million ethnic French returned to France, along with tens of thousands of *harkis*—Algerians who had worked for or fought for the French administration. It is now estimated that close to one million French are either *harki* emigrants or family of *harkis*. As such, the process of colonization and decolonization of Algeria transformed both countries culturally and ethnically. Although de Gaulle hoped that the granting of independence would help to maintain economic and political connections between the two countries, the animosity created by over a decade of war and brutality was overwhelming.

The new Algerian government, established as a one-party state under the FLN, announced a policy of Arab socialism and Pan-Arabism.

Decolonization in British sub-Saharan Africa

Although the British were willing to consider a rapid move to decolonization in locations such as India and Egypt, it is apparent that they had no such expectations for their colonies in sub-Saharan Africa. In part, this was because of British notions of race and development. But it was also because the British system of indirect rule treated every colony differently—based on the British understanding (often deeply flawed) of each population's economic, political, and cultural development. British colonial documents from immediately following World War II suggested that they saw independence for their colonies in Western and Eastern Africa as lying several decades in the future, at the soonest. They were deeply mistaken—for events in both in their colonies and in the wider world would shorten that timetable to little more than a single decade.

The fact that the British were so wrong about the future of their empire in Africa does not mean that they were unaware of the changing nature of the world. Indeed, the postwar British government (in part because of the ascent of the Labour Party to power) sought to extend greater sovereignty to African elites and even invested capital in African development to highlight the advantages of economic cooperation. These rather conservative reforms were a significant shift from prewar colonial policy, but were to be quickly overwhelmed by African initiative and associated global events in the late 1940s and 1950s. And nowhere was this initiative more dramatic than in the British West African colony of the Gold Coast, now known as Ghana.

The Gold Coast is an excellent example of how poorly popular stereotypes of Africa and colonialism represent historical reality. One of the world's largest gold producers, the region had been connected to the world economy for centuries—first through the trans-Saharan trade and later through the development of the Atlantic maritime connections (including the Atlantic slave trade). The interior was dominated by the Asante Empire in the eighteenth and nineteenth centuries and developed a strong sense of identity and the political organization and military might necessary to defeat British (and other) forces in the 1800s. On the coast, a cosmopolitan community of producers and merchants established economic, intellectual, and family ties throughout the region and the Atlantic world. During the early twentieth century local agriculturalists imported cocoa trees and launched a boom in production that made the Gold Coast the world's largest cocoa producer. By the postwar era, the Gold Coast was one of the wealthiest regions in the tropical world.

Residents of the Gold Coast, however, were aware that they had done more to benefit the British than the British had done to benefit them. This was particularly true in the wake of World War II, during which time Ghana had not only raised tens of thousands of troops (many of whom served in South Asia), but had also delivered significant quantities of gold, bauxite, and foodstuffs to the war effort. Indeed, a crucial turning point in the history of British colonialism in West Africa came in 1948, when a group of veterans of the Gold Coast Regiment marched to the British governor's residence to present a petition protesting the nonpayment of their military pensions and the rising cost of imported goods. Such protests were a common occurrence during the period as the nearly bankrupt colonial states failed to follow through on promised benefits for colonial servicemen. At the governor's residence they were fired on by a British police officer, and three servicemen were killed and many others were wounded. Popular discontent flared, and riots consumed the city for nearly a week.

Strikes, Protests, Riots, and Massacres in Postwar Africa

1944
November—Thiaroye Massacre: Thirty-five French African troops killed by French troops in Dakar, Senegal.

1945
May—Protestors in Sétif, Algeria, are fired on by French setters and troops. Riots break out and troops and settlers respond with greater violence. Thousands are killed.
June–August—General strikes in Nigeria.
September—Armed French settlers fire on African protesters in Doula, Cameroon. Twenty-one killed.
October—African railway workers strike in Northern and Southern Rhodesia.

1946
January—Strike in Dakar, Senegal, spreads through much of colony.
August—South African mineworkers strike.

1947
January—Dock workers in Mombasa, Kenya, and Dar es Salaam, Tanganyika, strike.
March—Beginning of nationalist uprising against French in Madagascar.
October—West African railway workers strike.
October—Workers in Gold Coast strike. Boycott of British goods.

1948
February—British police fire on African war veterans protesting nonpayment of benefits. Riots result. Twenty-nine killed.
July—General strike in Zanzibar.
October—General strike in Southern Rhodesia.

In response to the riots, the British arrested a number of members of the United Gold Coast Convention (UGCC), an organization of local elites who had organized to demand greater democratic representation of Africans within the Gold Coast government. Among those arrested was Kwame Nkrumah, who had recently returned from a decade of living in Britain and the United States. During that time, he was introduced to Marcus Garvey, C.L.R. James, and George Padmore's ideas of revolution and Pan-Africanism—eventually helping Padmore organize the 1945 Pan-African Congress in Manchester, England. Released several months later, many of the members of the UGCC were pleased with British constitutional reforms that promised universal suffrage and the formation of a Gold Coast parliament. However, Nkrumah saw the riots and British response as proof that even more rapid change was possible. Breaking with the UGCC, he formed his own Convention People's Party (CPP) and in 1950 called for a campaign of "Positive Action" in the form of strikes, civil disobedience, and mass rallies to demand an immediate independence for the Gold Coast. The British promptly rearrested Nkrumah. To their dismay, however, Nkrumah's CPP swept the scheduled 1951 election, and he went directly from jail to take the post of "head of government business"—famously wearing a cap with the letters "PG" to symbolize "Prison Graduate." By 1954 the Gold Coast, under Nkrumah's leadership, would gain full internal self-government and in March 1957 became an independent state.

The example of Ghana no doubt served as motivation for independence movements in other British colonies; populations and leaders elsewhere often found their own means to pressure the British for independence. Where possible, the British sought to balance their close working relationship with local political elites to temper the somewhat more radical demands made by nationalists who shared many intellectual and ideological perspectives with Nkrumah. For example, in Nigeria, the British worked carefully to set up a federal system of government that ensured the dominance of pro-British and aristocratic northern Muslim elites over the colony's more radical nationalist parties—including the National Council of Nigeria and the Cameroons (NCNC) led by Nnamdi Azikiwe and the Northern Elements Progressive Union (NEPU) led by Aminu Kano. A similar dynamic helped maintain the power of Mende elites in Sierra Leone.

As for their East African colonies, here the British expected independence to come somewhat more slowly than in West Africa. Even as Ghana and Nigeria moved to independence, the British Colonial Office suggested that independence in Kenya and Tanzania would not come until the 1970s at the earliest. In Kenya, this delay was in no small part due to the political influence of a small but economically and politically powerful population of white immigrants. Although nowhere near as numerous as the *colons* of Algeria, they nonetheless controlled the vast majority of the country's profitable coffee and tea production and enjoyed the rights of British citizenship denied to their African neighbors and workers. During the 1950s, the white seizure and control of the region's best agricultural lands was contested by a largely Kikuyu movement known as the Mau Mau. As in the case of the FLN, the Mau Mau attacked Europeans and those who worked with and for them. And, as in the case of Algeria, the initial colonial response was swift and brutal, with British forces incarcerating tens of thousands of Kikuyu and killing thousands in military scorched-earth campaigns, aerial bombardments, and through the widespread use of torture— including rape and castration.[2] It speaks volumes about the time that the British simultaneously were able to play on colonial racial stereotypes and popular fears by characterizing the Mau Mau movement as not a legitimate grievance among a people disposed of their land, but rather as ". . . an irrational force of evil, dominated by bestial impulses and influenced by world communism"[3].

---

[2] In 2013, the British government approved a payment of £14 million in compensation to some 5,000 Mau Mau detainees tortured by the British government. The payment, however, came without apology or official recognition of wrongdoing.

[3] Corfield, Frank. *The Origins and Growth of Mau Mau: an Historical Survey* (Nairobi: Government of Kenya 1960): p.5.

But even as the British were able to suppress the Mau Mau movement by 1956, they nonetheless became increasingly aware that the interests of a small population of British settlers could no longer outweigh the long-term interests of the British state, and they began to initiate a program of power transfer to the colony's African majority. Crucial to these negotiations was Jomo Kenyatta and his Kenya African National Union (KANU). Educated in Britain (and author of the famous emic ethnography *Facing Mt. Kenya*), Kenyatta had been jailed during the Mau Mau war as a subversive, though his alleged support for the rebellion has never been substantiated. Kenyatta was successful in easing the fears of white Kenyans and brokering a smooth transition to independence in 1963.

Decolonization in Francophone sub-Saharan Africa

French colonialism in Africa was in many ways distinct from that of the British. Unlike the British, the French established a common framework of administration known as direct rule and actively sought to assimilate Africans to French culture. Thus the French tended to be hostile to local elites and claimed to reward those Africans who embraced the French language, philosophy, and lifestyles. Indeed, the French had always claimed that their long-term goal was to incorporate their colonies and colonized populations into a "Greater France." By the postwar era some several thousand African *evolues* ("evolved Africans") had been granted full rights of citizenship. Like their counterparts in British colonies, however, most French African colonial subjects were unhappy with the slow pace of reform and felt that their contributions to the French during World War II had been illrewarded. This was especially true in French Equatorial Africa, which had been the lone holdout against the Vichy regime and had served as the refuge for the Free French leadership of de Gaulle until the defeat of the Vichy regime.

Many Francophone African leaders initially made an alliance with the French Communist Party, which in 1946 advocated full citizenship for all colonial subjects. In October of the same year, the French Communist Party sponsored the Bamako Congress, which led to the establishment of the *Rassemblement démocratique Africain* (African Democratic Party or RDA). The ruling French Socialist Party, however, sought to break the alliance between the French communists and the African leaders—arresting many leaders, banning meetings, and raising taxes on regions where communist support was strong. By 1950, most members of the RDA had broken with the communists. Chief among those to cross the carpet was Félix Houphouët-Boigny from the region of Côte d'Ivoire (the Ivory Coast). Yet, despite the shifts in political alliance, populations in French Africa continued to demand greater rights. In 1946, for example, the much-hated *Code de l'indigénat* (native code of law) was repealed. Indeed, the path to independence in French Africa was fairly rapid. As the historian Pat Manning pointed out, between 1945 and 1958 French Africans voted on four referenda, two constitutions, three National Assemblies, twice on the Assembly of the French Union, three times on the Federal Grand Council, and three times on the French Senate. Progress toward decolonization was not only a response to pressure from organizations such as the RDA, but was also a result of France's losing wars against independence movements in Vietnam and Algeria.

In 1958, all French colonies were given the opportunity to vote in a simple *Oui ou Non* (Yes or No) referendum on continued political and economic cooperation with France. Only Guinea, where the independence movement had been built around a strong labor union foundation, voted *non*. France sought to make an example of Guinea. They granted the country independence immediately, but did their best to punish the new state by destroying transportation, communications, and administrative infrastructure as they left—smashing the controls of the country's rail network, ripping telephones out of walls, burning government tax and census information, and even smashing the fine china at the governor's residence. These efforts pushed Guinea to promptly normalize relations with the Soviet Union and seek aid to keep the country afloat. The country's first president, Ahmed Sékou Touré, famously stated of the situation that "We prefer poverty in freedom to riches in slavery."

Despite their *oui* vote, most French African colonies received their independence in 1960. Independence for Djibouti, Mauritius, and the Comoros Islands was delayed by a decade or more in part because of these locations' strategic significance. Even with independence, however, France maintained relatively strong economic and political ties. Particularly notable was the maintenance of the CFA (*Communauté Financière Africaine*) franc, a currency common to all French West African and Central African states and backed by the French franc itself. The French, in agreement with the newly independent states, also maintained French troops at bases close to many of the new states' capitals. This gave the French government considerable leverage in the politics of the new states—a theme that will be developed in a later chapter.

There is much more to the story of African independence than just the ending of British and French colonial rule. In Chapter 3, "A Tropical Cold War," we will examine the movements for independence in Lusophone (Portuguese-speaking) Africa and also the struggle to end racist minority rule in Rhodesia and South Africa. Later in Chapter 3, we will also address the decolonization of Belgian Africa.

Global Liberation: Africa's Place in Worldwide Struggles for Sovereignty

As already mentioned, many African nationalists were inspired by the work of advocates for human rights and freedom elsewhere in the world. Marcus Garvey's Universal Negro Improvement Association (UNIA) was well known in most African cities, for example, as well as among Africans who had traveled to the Americas for work and education. As both the Civil Rights Movement and the push for African independence grew in the 1950s, the synergy between the two grew. In Ghana, for example, readers of the *Daily Graphic* newspaper were able to follow events pertaining to the movement in the United States, including the desegregation of the Little Rock school system, through reports sent back by Isaac Eshun, who visited Arkansas to cover the events for the newspaper.[4] Over the years, the paper also covered events such as the 1963 March on Washington and the passage of the Civil Rights Acts. Similarly, African-descended populations in the Americas followed the path of African states to independence. Martin Luther King attended the independence celebrations in Ghana and delivered sermons on the meaning of African independence for African Americans. W.E.B. DuBois immigrated to Ghana in 1963. Both cases highlight the parallels that many saw in the path to sovereignty in both the Americas and Africa.

But the awareness of global liberation movements was not confined by boundaries of "blackness" or "Africanness." Certainly the examples of independence in India and the Middle East played a crucial goal in inspiring African nationalists. Similarly, there was considerable cooperation between the nationalists' leadership of decolonizing and newly independent states in Africa and Asia. For example, in 1949 and 1955, delegates from Africa and Asia met in Bandung, Indonesia, to establish connections and set diplomatic strategy. The 1955 conference,

---

[4] Eshun, Isaac. "An 'on the Spot Study' of the Little Rock Scene." *Daily Graphic*, (July 7, 1959): p.5.

sometimes known as the Afro-Asian Conference, is famous for helping to establish the framework of the Non-Aligned Movement, which sought to create a block of nations that would align with neither the capitalist West nor the communist East in the Cold War. Rather, the goal was to create the option of an independent "Third World" that would advocate peace and development rather than vie for international dominance.

The movement for decolonization and sovereignty also coincided with the movement of indigenous peoples around the world. Groups as diverse as the Sami of northern Scandinavia and native populations in Guyana saw the similarity of their struggles for political equality and self-determination with populations in Africa. In the 1972 meeting of Non-Aligned Foreign Ministers, held in Georgetown, Guyana, was housed in a new meeting facility constructed by Wai-Wai Amerindians. The meeting also featured the unveiling of a monument featuring busts of Kwame Nkrumah, Gamal Nasser, Jawaharlal Nehru, and Josip Broz Tito.

The Quest for Unity and the Question of Unity

Calls for Pan-African unity had begun well before World War II. In the early twentieth century, most of these voices came from the African diaspora in North America and the Caribbean. In the postwar period, however, more and more African intellectuals began to take up the call for broader African cooperation and unity, encouraged and empowered in no small part by the rapid progress of numerous colonies toward political independence. The notion of a unified Africa was a powerful one. On the one hand, the idea was appealing in that a single African megastate would unavoidably wield considerable political and economic influence on a global scale. Similarly, a single African government would be able to utilize the resources of wealthier regions to develop more needy parts of the continent. Finally, the unification of Africa could also reflect a growing sense of African or perhaps even black identity that many (if not still far from most) of the continent's inhabitants were beginning to develop by the latter twentieth century. There were, however, numerous forces that acted against the impetus toward the dismantling of colonial boundaries and the formation of a broader African confederation or state.

Certainly one of the factors acting against wider African unity was the colonizers themselves. The British, French, Belgians, and Portuguese saw no advantage in the creation of a single African state.

Such a development would unavoidably water down the potential on-going influence of former colonial powers. Much the same was true for the superpowers of the United States and the Soviet Union.

Yet there were forces that were African in origin that also worked against the formation of a more unified Africa. For some, such as Houphouët-Boigny, the idea that the wealthier regions of Africa would fund the development of other parts of the continent was anathema. As a result, he worked, often in cooperation with the French, to help ensure that the sovereignty of wealthier regions such as Côte d'Ivoire would not be subjugated to a larger union—be that of a larger Francophone African states or a single African state. In contrast, Léopold Senghor worked to form a larger Mali Federation that combined the small and relatively wealthy region of Senegal with the much larger but less economically developed region of the French Sudan (now Mali). Senghor hoped that such a large federation would have greater political clout internationally. The Mali Federation, however, lasted little more than a year, and ended with the Senegalese detaining and deporting the political leaders from the French Sudan who had come to the new capital at Dakar. See Figure 1.1. A brief attempt to

FIGURE 1.1   Léopold Senghor and Félix Houphouët-Boigny

unify Senegal and Gambia (a British colony that nearly divided Senegal along the River Gambia) also failed. Such developments reflect the reality that creating a united Africa would demand that local political leaders surrender power and influence in order to create any sort of meaningful "African" government. Many found such an outcome unappealing.

Yet another challenge was the daunting challenge of creating a common African identity. Many of those living in the continent, especially those in rural areas or lacking extensive experience beyond the home region, had identities that were built around family, ethnicity, or religion. As such, the challenge of creating a new "national" identity was daunting enough for new governments. Put another way, the challenge of getting people to think of themselves as, say, "Zambian" or "Nigerian" was a major undertaking—a theme to which we will return in later chapters.

Despite all the forces working against unification, there were a few African leaders who nonetheless tried to make it a reality. Among these, there was no one who invested more in the quest for a united Africa than Kwame Nkrumah. There is not space available in this brief chapter to provide a detailed overview of Nkrumah's drive for Pan-Africanism, but a few brief examples may provide some insight into his efforts. First, Nkrumah worked energetically to foster close ties with Nasser in Egypt. Already calling for a Pan-Arab state, Nasser was also motivated to create a Pan-African union as well—a good example of the complex relationship and overlap between Africa and the Middle East. Perhaps nothing offers more insight into this relationship than the fact that Nkrumah took an Egyptian wife. In the long tradition of state marriages, the union of Kwame Nkrumah and Fathia Rizk (see Fig. 1.2) served more as a symbol of the connection between their countries than it did a personal bond. The two had never met before their marriage. Their first son was named Gamal in honor of Egypt's Nasser, though Fathia had no relationship to Nasser's family. On a broader scale, Nkrumah's quest for greater African unity is seen in his organization of the All-African People's Congress held in Accra, Ghana, in 1958, which brought together African nationalists and organizers from all across the continent.

A second example of Nkrumah's quest for greater African unity was his response to the "Congo Crisis." Belgium, unlike Britain and France, seemed unwilling to consider any form of expanded African sovereignty in the 1940s and 1950s. As a result, the Congolese had little

TOP: PREMIER WAVING AT THE AIRPORT YESTERDAY.
ABOVE: MRS NKRUMAH WAVING BACK TO HER HUSBAND.

FIGURE 1.2   Kwame and Fathia Nkrumah, from the *Daily Graphic*

or no opportunity to prepare for or gain experience in self-government. Fewer than a dozen Belgian Africans, for example, had received university degrees by 1960. Yet, when the Congolese awareness of decolonization elsewhere and frustration with Belgian intransigence exploded in protests and riots in 1959, the Belgians responded by rushing to allow elections and move to independence in June of 1960. In the elections, some 120 political parties contested for 137 seats in the parliament. The *Mouvement national congolaise* (MNC) won the largest number of seats (thirty-five) and formed a shaky coalition government with more than a dozen other parties. The MNC was led by Patrice Lumumba, who had met and formed a relationship with Nkrumah at the All-African People's Congress held in Accra just two years before. Like Nkrumah, Lumumba was a stanch Pan-Africanist who sought to avoid clear allegiance to either block in the Cold War.

The rush to independence in the Congo helped lay the foundation for little more than disaster. At the independence ceremony King Baudouin of Belgium waxed poetic about the benevolence of Belgian colonialism, a speech that brought this stinging rebuke from Lumumba:

> Although this independence of the Congo is being proclaimed today by agreement with Belgium, an amicable country, with which we are on equal terms, no Congolese will ever forget that independence was won in struggle, a persevering and inspired struggle carried on from day to day, a struggle, in which we were undaunted by privation or suffering and stinted neither strength nor blood. It was filled with tears, fire and blood. . . . That was our lot for the eighty years of colonial rule and our wounds are too fresh and much too painful to be forgotten. We have experienced forced labour in exchange for pay that did not allow us to satisfy our hunger, to clothe ourselves, to have decent lodgings or to bring up our children as dearly loved ones. Morning, noon and night we were subjected to jeers, insults and blows because we were "Negroes". Who will ever forget that the black was addressed as "*tu*", not because he was a friend, but because the polite "*vous*" was reserved for the white man?
> Long live independence and African unity!
> Long live the independent and sovereign Congo![5]

The independence and sovereignty of the Congo were soon to be challenged from within and without. Within days of independence, army mutinies, political divisions, and secession would begin to tear it

---

[5] Lumumba, Patrice, *The Truth about a Monstrous Crime of the Colonialists* (Moscow: Foreign Languages Publishing House, 1961): pp. 44–47.

apart. The Belgians supported the secession of the mineral-rich southern province of Katanga in July. In September, Lumumba's government was overthrown in a coup organized by Colonel Joseph Mobutu and supported by the US. Placed under house arrest, he later escaped and attempted to re-form his government. In December of 1960, Lumumba was captured by troops loyal to Mobutu. In January he was executed and his remains destroyed. Decades later it was revealed that the execution of Lumumba was carried out by Belgian agents, whose actions were known to the United States, whose own agents had attempted to poison Lumumba previously. Mobutu would continue to rule the Congo as a close American ally until the end of the Cold War.

Through the entire crisis, Nkrumah steadfastly demanded that the unity of the Congo be preserved—proof that he saw the future of Africa in larger, not smaller, units of governance. Nkrumah also lobbied extensively for an African-led military intervention to help reunify the new country and support Lumumba's government. He contributed Ghanaian forces to the UN effort there, for example, and then consistently condemned the UN for not responding with decisive military force. In August of 1960, a front-page story in the Ghanaian *Daily Graphic* newspaper quoted Nkrumah as stating that ". . . if given free reign, the Ghanaian troops would have the situation in Leopoldville back to normal in one week." In the years that followed, Nkrumah repeatedly cited the Congo Crisis as an example of how foreign powers could and would exploit the continent in the absence of African unity.

Nkrumah's call for a unified African government at the African Summit in 1963 is perhaps the best example of his dedication to Pan-Africanism. At the summit, he called for an African common market, a shared African currency and monetary zone supported by an African central bank, a single African citizenship, and a unified foreign policy. The following quotations are excerpts from his impassioned speech exhorting for the various newly independent African states to submit their newfound sovereignty to a unified Africa.

Early in the speech, Nkrumah spoke extensively of the ongoing power of European states and the ability of white minority governments in Southern Africa to deny sovereignty to African majorities:

> When Portugal violates Senegal's border, when Verwoerd allocates one-seventh of South Africa's budget to military and police, when France builds as part of her defense policy and interventionist force that can intervene . . . in French speaking

Africa, when Welensky talks of Southern Rhodesia joining South Africa, when Britain sends arms to South Africa, it is all part of a carefully calculated pattern working towards a single end: the continued enslavement of our dependent brothers and the onslaught upon the independence of our sovereign African states.

Do we have any other weapon against this design but our unity? Is not our unity essential to guard our own freedom as well as to win freedom for our oppressed brothers the freedom fighters? Is it not unity alone that can weld us into an effective force capable of creating our own progress and making our valuable contribution to world peace?

He then moved on to discuss the political and economic problems created by colonial boundaries:

There is hardly an African state without a frontier problem with its adjacent neighbors . . . let me suggest to Your Excellencies that this fatal relic of colonialism will drive us to war against one another as our unplanned and uncooperative industrial development expands, just as happened in Europe. Only African unity can heal this festering sore of boundary disputes between our various states. Your Excellencies, the remedy for these ills is ready to our hand. It stares us in the face at every customs barrier. It shouts to us from every African heart.

Nkrumah then concluded by highlighting the potential of a unified Africa to serve as an example to a world divided and threatened by the Cold War:

If we in Africa can achieve the example of a continent knit together in common policy and common purpose, we shall have made the finest possible contribution to that peace for which all men and women thirst today. And which will lift once again and forever the deepening shadow of global destruction from mankind. AFRICA MUST UNITE!

Despite Nkrumah's impassioned plea, the outcome of the African Summit was far less dramatic than he hoped for (see Fig. 1.3). Rather than any sort of unified state, the outcome was the creation of a loose "Organization of African Unity" that did little more than outline a shared interest in development and freedom from Cold War entanglements. Greater common support was established to work for the freedom of populations in Portuguese African and under white minority rule in Rhodesia and South Africa. More attention will be given to these topics in Chapter 3.

Leaders take the historic decision

MONDAY,   MAY 27, 1963.   No. 3937

AFRICA
IS NOW ONE!

Ceremonial welcome awaits Kwame today

ONE Africa is born . . . ! This was marked by the signing of the "Charter of Unity" signed by 30 African Heads of State and Government at a historic ceremony held in Africa Hall, Addis Ababa, Ethiopia, at the week-end.

The ceremony was the climax of four days of talks by African heads including Osagyefo Dr Nkrumah.

Applauded by their colleagues the 30 heads of state signed one by one the historic charter setting up a common assembly, meeting once a year, and a permanent secretariat.

The African leaders decided to settle all differences among themselves peacefully through a mediation, conciliation and arbitration commission.

Only two of the 32 leaders of independent African states were missing when the documents were signed. Reuter reported.

Standing ovation for Osagyefo

FIGURE 1.3   "Africa is Now One," headline from the *Daily Graphic*

CONCLUSION—VICTORIES ACHIEVED AND CHALLENGES TO COME

Even without the creation of a Pan-African state, it was hard in 1960s to see the achievement of African independence as anything other than progress. What was not to be embraced about greater sovereignty? About independence? Freedom? About the defeat of overseas colonial masters? The victories of so many new African states over European colonial powers resonated with populations in America, the Soviet Union, and elsewhere in the decolonized and decolonizing world. The transformation of Africa tells us much about how the world was dramatically changing in the second half of the twentieth century. As Nkrumah said early in his demands for independence in Ghana, "Seek ye first the political kingdom, and all else shall be added unto you." But, as we shall see in the coming chapters, the conquest of the political kingdom did not necessarily ensure that "all else" would be added so easily. As almost all African rulers and populations were soon to learn, maintaining a sovereign state is often every bit as difficult, if not sometimes even more so, as gaining independence. Similarly, the quest for economic development was also a far more complex process than pretty much anyone, in Africa or elsewhere, thought. Further, there remained the struggle for independence in states where those in power were far less willing to relinquish power freely—and where the international politics of the Cold War were all the more harsh.

REFERENCES AND FURTHER READINGS

Anderson, David. *Histories of the Hanged: The Dirty War in Kenya and the End of Empire* (New York: Norton, 2013).

Azikiwe, Nnamdi. *Zik: Selected Speeches of Dr. Nnamdi Azikiwe* (Cambridge, UK: Cambridge University Press, 1961).

Cartey, Wilfred and Martin Kilson. *The African Reader: Independent Africa* (New York: Vintage Books, 1970).

Enwezor, Okwui, Ed. *The Short Century: Independence and Liberation Movements in Africa 1945–1994* (New York: Prestel, 2001).

Hargreaves, J.D. *Decolonization in Africa* (New York: Longman, 1996).

Kenyatta, Jomo. *Facing Mt. Kenya* (New York: Vintage Books, 1962).

Le Sueur, James D. *The Decolonization Reader* (Florence, KY: Routledge, 2003).

Manning, Patrick. *Francophone Sub-Saharan Africa: 1880–1995* (Cambridge, UK: Cambridge University Press, 1999).

Shepard, Todd. *The Invention of Decolonization: The Algerian War and the Remaking of France* (Cornell, NY: Cornell University Press, 2008).

Wallerstein, Immanuel. *Africa: The Politics of Independence* (New York: Vintage Books, 1961).

Development and Debt

INTRODUCTION: THE IDEA OF AFRICAN DECLINE AND DECAY

Several years ago, I happened to be working on a presentation to give to local schools and organizations about common American "notions of Africa." One of the notions was what I've come to call "Broken Africa"—the idea that nothing in Africa ever really works and things constantly get worse, rather than better. In looking for images to go with the various concepts, I happened to find a graphic that was, frankly, depressing. It was a simple picture of Africa superimposed upon a grid with a red arrow charting some generic decline. There was no counterimage available representing progress in such a simple and direct manner.[1]

Such an image is representative of how all too many people outside of Africa, especially in wealthier countries, view the continent. One of the jobs of historians, however, is to point out that

---

[1] In istockphoto.com's defense, this image is no longer in their inventory. Indeed, as a reflection of the recent economic boom in much of Africa, there are now a number of more positive images.

contemporary images are not always accurate—or are at least far more complicated than most people think they are. Indeed, for much of the twentieth century, most people thought of Africa as a land of progress. Colonial powers justified much of their power on the grounds that they were helping to develop the continent and its peoples. Likewise, when many African states gained independence in the 1950s and 1960s, one of the core ambitions of the political leadership was to use their newfound economic sovereignty to develop new industries and bring wealth and quality of life to their citizens. As such, this chapter examines this era of optimism and exuberance, as well as the period of disillusionment that followed all too close on its heels. The chapter then closes on a somewhat more optimistic note by examining the roots of the economic boom that much of the continent is experiencing in the current day. Along the way, the chapter looks at the global context of African development and briefly examines the various economic strategies employed by different African states. In so doing, this chapter seeks to provide a more balanced perspective on both the successes and failures of African economic development in the period from the late 1950s through the early 1990s.

BACKGROUND: THE ECONOMIC LEGACY OF COLONIALISM AND CONCEPTS OF DEVELOPMENT

As just noted, most colonial powers made rather a big deal out of their alleged contributions to African development. As a result, inhabitants of the industrialized world often think of colonialism in terms of benevolence. It is not at all unusual for students in America or France, for example, to think that European colonizers "built roads" in Africa. These same students are also often somewhat surprised to find out that most Africans (and African history professors) tend to see things somewhat differently. Although it is certainly the case that colonial rule changed the course of African economic development, the nature of that development is rather more complex. In short, the sort of economic development brought by colonialism was narrowly focused on extracting and exporting agricultural and mineral resources at the lowest possible cost and maintaining African populations as consumers of finished goods manufactured in Europe. Keeping these costs low meant that Africans, rather than Europeans, not only did the work to build those roads, but they paid for them through their labor, taxes, and the service of loans taken out by colonial governments. Under colonialism, many Africans became engaged in the global economy, but the profits from their production of cash crops or other goods for export and their purchase of finished goods from abroad mostly benefited Europeans. Moreover, colonial administrations often sought to suppress African manufacturing, because Africans who made their own cloth, iron, soap, or whatnot, were not as likely to buy similar goods from the colonizing country. Such an economic framework is not exactly what those living in industrialized countries think of as "development." Indeed, in his influential and controversial work *How Europe Underdeveloped Africa*, Walter Rodney, one of the founders of modern-day African studies, argued the slave trade and colonialism had, together, served to undermine African economic and industrial progress.[2]

In the mid-twentieth century, the idea of development and progress really meant only one thing, and that was industrialization. Industry meant many things. It meant producing the stuff other things are made of, such as steel for bridges and chemicals for paints or medicines. It meant that many and sometimes even most people lived in cities and worked making things rather than living in the countryside growing things to eat. Industrialized countries tended to be relatively wealthy and militarily powerful. Industrialization meant sovereignty. As such, industrialization was seen as something to be desired. Some even celebrated the environmental costs—defining the destruction of forests and the pollution of rivers as the "march of progress."

---

[2] Rodney, 1972.

THEORIES OF ECONOMIC DEVELOPMENT AT MID-CENTURY

In such a context, it is hardly any surprise that as African states began to move toward independence in the 1950s and 1960s, their leadership and citizens aspired to economic as well as political sovereignty. The question, of course, was, how would such development be achieved? Few were so naive as to think it would happen all by itself. But just as there was general agreement in the mid-twentieth century that industrialization was a good thing, there was also strong consensus among politicians and economists of how economic growth was best facilitated—and that was through direct state intervention.

This notion of state-directed development was shared across a number of different ideological perspectives. The strongest example for the efficacy of the state in directing development came from the Soviet Union. In this case, a radical transformation of the Russian political and economic system had taken a largely agrarian state with limited industry and a weak military and turned it into a "superpower" in roughly three decades. Indeed, the emergence of the Soviet Union as a state not only capable of defending itself from Nazi Germany but also of launching the first artificial satellite and first human into space was a powerful example of the potential for countries to achieve rapid industrialization and gain prominence on the global stage.

Even in the United States and Western Europe, the crises of the Great Depression had demanded a substantial degree of government involvement to facilitate economic recovery. These ideas were reinforced by the work of the British economist John Maynard Keynes, who argued that government intervention could stop or at least soften the boom and bust cycles that had plagued Western economies in the modern era. The success of the Tennessee Valley Authority (TVA) project in the United States in helping to bring electricity and industrial development to one of the poorest and least-developed parts of the United States was often cited as a case of successful state intervention even in a "capitalist" context. Other cases include the influence of the Eisenhower interstate system in facilitating economic growth in the United States and the role of the government in expanding higher education under the G.I. Bill.

Indeed, as European countries sought to recover from the ravages of World War II, there was little or no talk of "leaving the market to fix things." Supported by the US Marshall Plan, European states undertook extensive government investment in infrastructure and industry to rebuild and to facilitate economic recovery. European states such as Britain moved to nationalize key sectors of the economy, including mining, electrical production, and health care. In general, the results were dramatic, with Germany and France, for example, posting significant rates of economic growth in the decade after the end of the war.

CASE STUDIES OF ECONOMIC DEVELOPMENT: GHANA, CÔTE D'IVOIRE, AND TANZANIA

Given the history of economic exploitation under colonialism and also the general confidence in state-managed development that character-ized international economic thinking in mid-century, it should come as no surprise that African leaders (and a host of international economic "advisors") expressed support for government involvement in economic development. The level of confidence in such measures was high. Fur-ther, this enthusiasm was far from unfounded. Beyond the apparent efficacy of state-directed development "proven" by the model of the Soviet Union and US and European recovery before and after the war, the growing global economy also created a boom in demand for African commodities such as cocoa, coffee, tea, palm oil, and others. This boom was accompanied by a serendipitous period of favorable weather across much of the continent in the decades after the war. Year after year the rains came on time and provided neither too much nor too little water, helping to create bumper crops of both cash and food crops.

This climate of optimism for rapid economic transformation and development was certainly present in newly independent Ghana. Wit-ness the following speech made by Kwame Nkrumah during the new country's independence celebration:

> Ghana inherited a colonial economy. . . . We cannot rest until we have demolished this miserable structure and raised in its place an edifice of economic stability thus creating for ourselves a veritable paradise of abundance and satisfaction. . . . We must go forward with our preparations for planned economic growth to supplant the poverty, ignorance, disease and illiteracy left in the wake of discredited colo-nialism and decaying imperialism. . . . Socialism is the only pattern that can within the shortest possible time bring the good life to the people.

There seemed to have been plenty of reason for Nkrumah's opti-mism. Far from isolated, Ghana had a long history of engagement with the global economy. Among the world's largest producers of gold, bauxite, cocoa, and kola, it was one of the wealthiest tropical countries in the world, with substantial reserves of "hard" currency and, especially in the south, a significant population of educated and cosmopolitan professionals. Nkrumah and other Ghanaian leaders, however, were not content to rely only on extractive industries such as mining and agriculture for wealth. As such, the newly independent country launched a host of development programs that reflected what has come to be known as a "structuralist" model of development—a program aimed at creating an industrialized Ghana that was both more economically independent and internationally competitive (see Fig. 2.1).

Infrastructure, essential to the creation of a thriving national economy, was a major focus of investment. Regional administrations and the national government each spent substantial sums on the construction of roads and bridges. A deep-water harbor (almost no natural harbors exist along Africa's Atlantic coast) was constructed at Tema and opened in 1962. Simultaneously, the Ghanaian government established the "Black Star Line" of shipping vessels so as to not be dependent on other countries for the import and export of goods.

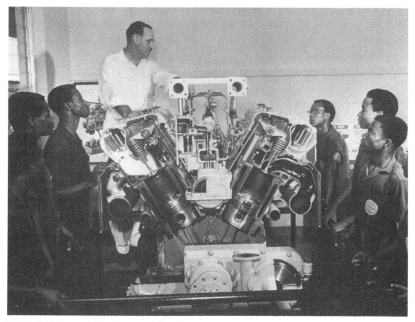

FIGURE 2.1   Nigerian mechanics

In particular, however, the new Ghanaian government believed that industrialization was the only possible path toward true economic sovereignty and prosperity. This drive is well represented in a newspaper editorial from 1963, titled "The Problems of Industrialization: Planning the Priorities":

> Industrialization has become a blessed word, not only in Ghana, but also in all the newly independent countries of Africa. These countries are eager to transform their lop-sided development and servile dependence on others (especially their former colonial masters) into a balanced development and honourable interdependency. A diamond producing country like Ghana, which has no diamond polishing and cutting industry, is depriving itself of the best part of the sauce.[3]

On the consumer level, the government undertook a policy known as "import substitution," which focused on producing in Ghana manufactured goods currently being imported from outside. Progress on this front was lauded by government officials in speeches and celebrated in newspaper stories. In an editorial titled "Made in Ghana" in 1962, the article listed the new products being produced in Ghana:

> In less than six years after independence, Ghana now produces her own safety matches, paints, nails, biscuits, alcoholic drinks, cooking utensils, roofing materials, canned fruits, meat and fish, and has her own chemical factory for producing insecticides and chemicals.[4]

Ghana also sought to produce more substantial and potentially productive products. The Ghana Boatyards Corporation, for example, was established to build not only fishing boats to bolster the country's maritime economy, but also pleasure craft for export. The sale of several dozen small sailing boats to a New Orleans' yacht club in 1962, for example, was given considerable attention and celebrated as evidence of the ability of Ghanaian companies to compete internationally. In cooperation with the British United Africa Company, a truck factory was established in 1959 for the assembly of Bedford trucks from parts imported from Britain. The goal here was to develop both the skills of automotive manufacture and maintenance so as to allow Ghana to develop its own car and truck industries in the future. In this vein, it

---

[3] "The Problems of Industrialization: Planning the Priorities," *Daily Graphic*, August 2, 1963, p. 5.

[4] "Made in Ghana, Part Two," *Daily Graphic*, November 30, 1962, p. 9.

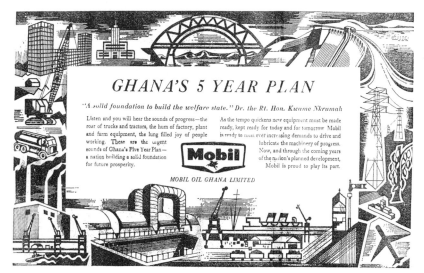

FIGURE 2.2   "Ghana's 5-Year Plan," from the *Daily Graphic*

is important to note that Ghana's state-directed approach for development and frequent references to socialism did not mean that the country was opposed to foreign investment, or that manufacturing concerns from abroad were unwilling to cooperate with socialist Ghana (see Fig. 2.2). As one advertisement taken out by Kumasi Breweries Limited (backed by British investors) stated, "Kumasi Breweries Limited is proud to play its part in the planned prosperity of Ghana" and went on to list how the company was helping Ghana develop by training technicians and managers (see Fig. 2.3).

Such internal production of consumer goods was of crucial importance to emerging economies because of how the international monetary system works. The purchase of goods from outside the country necessitated the acquisition and spending of "hard currencies"—the money issued by established industrial economies. Currencies like the Ghanaian cedi were (and still are) considered "soft" and "nonconvertible," that is, they could not be used for international trade. Thus, purchasing soap or matches manufactured in Britain meant spending a limited store of British pounds that could be acquired only by selling goods (usually unprocessed agricultural or mineral goods) to the British. Thus manufacturing and using one's own soap meant saving hard currency that could be invested in more productive ways.

FIGURE 2.3　"Star Beer," from the *Daily Graphic*

The most ambitious undertaking by the new Ghanaian state was the Volta River Project and the associated Volta Aluminum Company (Valco). Modeled in no small part on the creation of hydroelectric dams constructed by the TVA in the American south and the use of that power to build the world's largest aluminum smelting plant at Alcoa in Tennessee and also by Egypt's Aswan High Dam (see Fig. 2.4), the project set out to create the world's largest human-engineered lake by means of the damming of the Volta River at Akosombo. The electricity produced by this massive undertaking would then be used not only to meet much of Ghana's growing public demand for power, but also to run a massive aluminum smelting factory that would allow Ghana to export processed aluminum rather than unprocessed bauxite ore. Most of the capital for the dam came from the Ghanaian government, whereas Valco was established and operated largely by the US Reynolds Aluminum Company. The dam was completed in 1965, and production of aluminum at Valco began in 1967—a year after the overthrow of Kwame Nkrumah by a military coup.

Significantly, the Convention People's Party (CPP) invested little in Ghana's agricultural production. A few collective farms were established as an experiment in more technically intensive agriculture, but for the most part farmers received little support from this industrially oriented administration. Rather, the Ghanaian government treated farmers, especially those growing cash crops such as cocoa, as a source of revenue. As a result, even as cocoa prices boomed in the 1950s, prices to producers remained low so that the government could sell the cocoa at a profit and use the hard currency earned to finance more "modern" development in industry. Indeed, from the perspective of the farmers, the new Ghanaian government treated them little differently than had the colonial administration. As cocoa prices collapsed in the 1960s, the government cut producer prices even more sharply, adding significantly to the growing discontent with Nkrumah and his CPP administration.

If one were to seek an example of a country that charted a different path to development than Ghana, one would need look no farther than the neighboring Côte d'Ivoire (the Ivory Coast). Both countries shared similar physical environments, and, like Ghana, Côte d'Ivoire had developed a modest degree of wealth from agricultural exports, in this case to France Although once allied to the French Communist Party, Côte d'Ivoire's first president Félix Houphouët-Boigny took a far more conservative path toward development following independence than his neighbor and frequent rival Kwame Nkrumah. Their very

FIGURE 2.4 Soviet premier Nikita Khrushchev and Egyptian leader Gamal Abdel Nasser tour the Aswan High Dam

different approaches to development famously took the form of a bet offered by Houphouët-Boigny during a visit by Nkrumah to the Côte d'Ivoire in 1957. Disagreeing on both the best path to development and the proper nature of relations with former colonial rulers, Houphouët-Boigny offered, "So let us meet up again in ten years to see who among us has chosen the best approach for his people."

Rejecting a drive for rapid industrialization, Houphouët-Boigny instead chose to invest heavily in agricultural production—particularly in cash crops. Like Ghana, the Côte d'Ivoire was a major cocoa exporter, and the new administration sought to encourage still more cocoa production, both by local producers and international investors. The government also subsidized the creation of coffee plantations and encouraged the expansion of exports of pineapples, bananas, kola nuts, latex, timber, and cotton. The result was an expansion of the Côte d'Ivoire's export earnings that averaged nearly 12 percent per year well into the 1970s.

In no small part, the Côte d'Ivoire's success came from substantial foreign investment. Houphouët-Boigny's criticism of anticolonial rhetoric and stress on the "fraternal" relationship with France, combined with numerous tax breaks for foreign companies, created a "business friendly environment." Just as France punished Guinea for breaking with their former colonial ruler, the French sought to use the Côte d'Ivoire as an example of the benefits of continued cooperation. Not only did French investment and aid flow into the Côte d'Ivoire, but so did French people. By the 1970s a substantial portion of the Côte d'Ivoire's civil service was staffed by French bureaucrats. And although the Ivorian government showed little interest in industrial growth, many French companies established light industries for the production of processed foods and some consumer items. In 1968, French companies remitted some US$34 million in profits back to France—more than double the French "aid" offered to the Côte d'Ivoire. As a result, decolonization in the Côte d'Ivoire meant that more French, rather than fewer, were to be found in the new country. Happy to play the contrarian, Houphouët-Boigny once stated, "If I could have twice as many Frenchmen as we have to help us build the Ivory Coast, I would take them."

The Côte d'Ivoire's gains were very real. Production of cocoa soon surpassed that of Ghana. In fact, by the 1960s, Ghanaian cocoa farmers were smuggling their products to the Côte d'Ivoire in order to take advantage of the higher prices offered there. Per capita income grew at nearly 10 percent per year, raising Ivorian earnings to the second highest in Africa (behind those of South Africa). High levels of production also created a demand for labor. Nearly a million migrants, mostly from Burkina Faso to the north and Guinea to the west, moved to the Côte d'Ivoire to take positions as agricultural workers. With the CFA (*Communauté Financière Africaine*) shared by Côte d'Ivoire and all other former French African colonies (except Guinea) backed by the French franc, Ivorians were also insulated from the high rates of inflation faced by their Ghanaian neighbors, allowing them to more easily purchase manufactured goods from abroad. Observers dubbed the country's progress "The Ivorian Miracle."

At the ten-year mark after Houphouët-Boigny and Nkrumah's famous wager, there seemed little doubt over who had won the bet. In its bid for rapid industrial development (and pan-African unity), Ghana had run up substantial debts—with some investments producing little or even negative financial return. Further, having responded to growing popular discontent with crackdowns on even the slightest opposition and the creation of an overbearing "cult of personality," Nkrumah was overthrown in a military coup in February of 1966 and on the tenth anniversary of the bet was living in exile in Guinea.[5] Ghanaians' standard of living had dropped precipitously, even as Ivorians' saw substantial gains. The story of the comparative development of Ghana and the Côte d'Ivoire does not end here, however, and we will revisit the subject later in this chapter.

A final case study of the drive for economic independence takes us to East Africa—in this case to the country now known as Tanzania.[6] Here the government charted a path to development that was distinct from that of either Ghana or the Côte d'Ivoire. In so doing, Tanzania rejected the notion of rapid industrialization, but also rejected the idea that foreign investment and cash cropping were the best means to development. First ruled by the Germans and later by the British, the colony of Tanzania differed from Ghana and the Côte d'Ivoire in many other ways as well. First, the region was sparsely populated and possessed a much smaller economy—agricultural or otherwise. With less of a legacy in production and trade with the industrialized world, the new country possessed little in the way of infrastructure, capital,

---

[5] To add insult to injury, Houphouët-Boigny provided material and logistical aid to the Ghanaian military officers who overthrew Nkrumah.

[6] Under the British, the colony was known as Tanganyika. Following the union with the island of Zanzibar in 1964, the independent country changed its name to Tanzania.

or a "cosmopolitan" elite with experience in Western-style management or governance. Nonetheless, during the 1960s, under the leadership of Julius Nyerere and the Tanzanian African National Union (TANU), Tanzania was to become something of a darling of international development specialists and political progressives alike. In no small part, this attention was a result of Nyerere's personal charm and political savvy, much of which came together in his program of "African Socialism."

In developing the concept of "African Socialism," Nyerere stressed that collective labor and self-reliance (*ujamaa*) were already core elements of African culture and thus were strategies that were independent of Cold War ideological entanglements. Nyerere sought to rely on local labor and skills to develop a modern agricultural economy at minimum expense while providing as many modern services as possible to the country's far-flung population. In so doing, Nyerere hoped to "build the nation" in terms of creating a Tanzanian identity at the same time as a new economy was being established. Quite opposed to the approach taken by Nkrumah, Nyerere was also comfortable with a slower path to development if so doing better maintained Tanzania's newfound independence. In the 1960s, Tanzania was considered a very cool place. Witness the following newspaper editorial by Basil Davidson, one of the founders of African Studies:

> Far off the beaten track I have bumped and thumped in my Land Rover into the most remote villages and found the TANU flag flying proudly on a high pole beside a TANU office that may often be little more than a mud-walled hut. This is grassroots democracy in the truest meaning of the word. It can be seen that Nyerere and his fellow-ministers are actively and purposefully engaged in the exacting job of causing Tanganyika to raise itself 'by its own bootstraps.'[7]

Although Nyerere and others spoke of *ujamaa* frequently during the early 1960s, it was the Arusha Declaration of February 1967 that both codified Tanzania's unique strategy for development and secured the country's "cutting edge" status in terms of the quest for development and social justice. In particular, the Arusha Declaration hoped to create a framework for economic and political development that would lift up all Tanzanians equally and not create the sort of hierarchy of

---

[7] Davidson, Basil, "Tanganyika on a Firm Basis," *Daily Graphic*, December 28, 1962, p. 5.

wealth and class that would empower a small minority and disadvantage the majority. As one section of the Declaration stated,

> A truly socialist state is one in which all people are workers and in which neither capitalism nor feudalism exists. It does not have two classes of people, a lower class composed of people who work for their living, and an upper class of people who live on the work of others. In a really socialist country no person exploits another; everyone who is physically able to work does so; every worker obtains a just return for the labour he performs; and the incomes derived from different types of work are not grossly divergent.[8]

To this end, the Arusha Declaration resulted in the nationalization of many aspects of the Tanzanian economy, including banking, import and export companies, and manufacturing.

The most important components of this strategy of development, however, were to be "Ujamaa Villages." The nature of these villages was described by Nyerere:

> Their community would be the traditional family group, or any other group of people living according to *ujamaa* principles, large enough to take account of modern methods and the twentieth century needs of man. The land this community farmed would be called 'our land' by all the members; the crops they produced on that land would be 'our crop'; it would be 'our shop' which provided individual members with the day-to-day necessities from outside; 'our workshop' which made the bricks from which houses and other buildings were constructed, and so on.[9]

Underpinning the idea of the Ujamaa Villages was the belief that extending infrastructure and services such as roads, water, sanitation, power, education, and health care to all existing villages would be too expensive for the young state to bear. Instead, people would voluntarily reorganize themselves or relocate to the new Ujamaa Villages, which would be both larger and ideally more strategically located so as to more easily provide for the needs of the population. Similarly, because of the communal nature of the farming undertaken by these new villages, technology in the form of tractors, fertilizers, pesticides, and the like could more easily be distributed so as to

---

[8] Arusha Declaration, February 5, 1967. Available at http://www.fordham.edu/halsall/mod/1967-arusha.html

[9] Minogue and Molloy, 1974, p. 90.

facilitate expansions in production, which would create wealth for the community and the nation.

In the first five years of the program, however, most Tanzanians seemed ill-inclined to establish or move to the new Ujamaa Villages. Many did not want to leave their established homes and communitics. Others doubted the ability of the government to fulfill its promises. At first the government attempted to make the Ujamaa Villages more appealing by giving their inhabitants preference in terms of access to government services. When this too failed to encourage the majority of the population to take part, Nyerere announced in 1973 that the creation of communal villages was mandatory. Over the next few years some 11 million Tanzanians were forcibly relocated to communal farms. In some cases, abandoned homes and towns were destroyed so as to prevent populations from returning. Worse, the management of the relocations was often poorly organized, and people found themselves relocated to Ujamaa Villages that existed largely only in name.

The results were devastating on a variety of levels. Between 1974 and 1977 food production dropped dramatically, and Tanzania was forced to appeal to international organizations and donor nations for emergency deliveries of staple foods to prevent famine. The Tanzanian government was forced to take out significant loans in order to maintain basic service and meet payrolls for government officials. The Tanzanian standard of living, already low by global standards, declined significantly as well. But perhaps most devastating was the blow to the Tanzanians' faith in their own government and sense of optimism in the future.

DROUGHT AND DEBT— AFRICA IN THE 1970s AND 1980s

It is a common theme of mainstream accounts of Africa since independence, both those produced in and outside of Africa, to place the blame for African economic woes at the feet of African leaders. Certainly no small amount of evidence suggests that any number of poor choices were made by African politicians in the quest for development or status—a few of which have already been noted here. This approach, however, does have the danger of suggesting that African leaders were either somehow less intelligent than politicians elsewhere in the world or were not faced by challenges that were in some ways unique.

Indeed, the cases of Ghana, the Côte d'Ivoire, and Tanzania provide some insight into the trajectory of the economies of many other African states in the decades following independence. By and large, most states saw their economies grow throughout the 1960s, though Ghana perhaps provides a cautionary tale of spending too much too fast in pursuit of rapid development. In the 1970s, however, the fate of most, though not all, African economies took a turn decidedly for the worse. Crucially, many of the reasons for these economic stresses were international or environmental in nature.

Beginning in the 1960s, the "boom" of the postwar era began to slow. One of the first shocks was a sudden decline in cocoa prices, brought on in part by surging production not only in West Africa, but also from new producer countries such as Brazil. New and cheaper sources of bauxite from Jamaica and Australia led to a collapse in prices for the mineral. It speaks volumes about the complexity of global markets that the US companies running the Valco smelter found it cheaper to produce aluminum in Ghana with ore imported from Jamaica than to use Ghanaian ore. Although not as sudden, the prices earned for many other agricultural and mineral commodities also declined. Ghana was hit particularly hard by the drop in revenue. The Côte d'Ivoire was able to adapt in part because coffee prices remained high during the 1960s and 1970s.

A much broader and more severe shock came as a result of international politics in 1973. Following the 1973 Arab-Israeli War, Arab countries launched an oil embargo to protest Western support for Israel. As a consequence, global prices for crude oil and refined gasoline skyrocketed. The Oil Crisis of the 1970s was powerful enough to tumble the US stock market and throw even the world's richest countries into recession. The impact in Africa (and elsewhere in the developing world) was even more crushing. The vast majority of African states were (and remain today) dependent on imports of petroleum products not only to run vehicles, but also in the form of kerosene to fuel stoves and lamps and diesel fuel to generate electricity. Further, because a host of chemicals, fertilizers, and plastics are petroleum based, costs for crucial agricultural and medical supplies also rose. In 1972 fuel imports cost Tanzania nearly 10 percent of its annual export revenue. By the late 1970s, the country was spending roughly half of its hard currency on imported petroleum. In comparison, the United States has never spent more than 3 percent of its gross domestic product (GDP) on petroleum imports, even though it consumes significantly more fuel on a per capita basis than any other country in the world.

Yet another element of the storm that buffeted African economies in the 1970s was the global environment itself. Beginning with a
devastating drought that struck a swath of Africa from the Senegam-
bia in the west to the Horn of Africa in the east from 1973 to 1974 and
with additional droughts hitting these and other regions in the early
1980s, and 1990s. Food and cash crop production was devastated in
many regions, sometimes for years in a row. As a result, countries that
had struggled to increase agricultural production to earn hard currency and feed growing populations, often in the face of competition
with cheap imports of heavily subsidized grain from the United States
and Europe, found themselves forced to import not only expensive
petroleum products, but also larger and larger quantities of foodstuffs.
Countries such as Ghana and Nigeria, which had invested heavily in
hydroelectric power, saw lake levels drop so low that electrical production had to be halted.

The impact of the economic crises of the 1970s was not simply
limited to a rising cost of fuel and demand for expanded food imports.
Indeed, even money itself became more expensive during this time.
Faced with recession and high inflation by the mid-1970s, the Carter
administration in the United States began raising interest rates so as
to encourage savings and discourage spending on imported goods. By
1980, US Federal interest rates had peaked at roughly 18 percent,
with consumer mortgages and loans exceeding 20 percent. Because of
the influence of US financial policy on a global scale, however, these
actions meant that the interest rates of loans taken out by developing
states also increased significantly—even as fuel prices skyrocketed
and droughts undercut agricultural production. Thus, just as economic
misfortune forced African states to borrow to keep economies and
services moving, the cost of that borrowing increased substantially.
As a result, national debts, which had remained relatively small
during the 1960s, began to balloon during the 1970s and had grown
to crisis levels by the 1980s.

In Ghana, already stressed by ambitious development projects
and falling cocoa revenues, the rise in import costs and interest rates
led to near-total economic collapse. Exports dropped as farmers saw
little value in working to produce cash or food crops that earned so
little capital in return for hard labor. Prices for increasingly scarce
imported goods skyrocketed. The government attempted to cope with
price controls and by maintaining an artificially high value for the cedi,
but these policies served mostly to create a booming black market and a
"dual economy" that benefited those few (mostly political insiders) with

access to hard currency. Tanzania, never wealthy to begin with, struggled under the hammer blows of drought, fuel costs, and the wildly unpopular Ujamaa Village program.

Even the Côte d'Ivoire, which had seemed to have done everything "right" in the 1960s and early 1970s, faced growing problems by the 1980s. Prices for commodities began to fall across the board as global production and competition, particularly from other tropical regions such as Southeast Asia and Latin America, grew. As a result, the Côte d'Ivoire's economy fell into sharp recession in the 1980s, shrinking by more than a quarter. At the same time, however, Houphouët-Boigny seemed determine to establish his own legacy through the construction of massive edifices such as one of the world's largest cathedrals and by moving the nation's capital to his home town of Yamoussoukro. Worse, as the economic situation worsened, tensions began to grow between "indigenous" Ivorians and the millions of migrants, mostly from Burkina Faso to the north, who had emigrated to work in the country's expanding agricultural sector during previous decades.

OIL BOOMS AND BUSTS

It is important to note that the 1970s were not a disaster everywhere in Africa. In particular, oil-producing countries such as Algeria, Libya, Nigeria, Gabon, and Angola saw economic booms. Nigeria's significant reserves of "Bonny Light" sweet crude (which is particularly cheap to refine) were beginning to be exported in significant quantities just as global oil prices surged in the early 1970s. As a result, Nigeria experienced a boom economy of epic proportions even as her neighbors suffered. Indeed, ask Nigerians about the 1970s and they will often smile and sigh wistfully. As the national budget expanded from hundreds of millions to tens of billions of dollars in size, the Nigerian government went into a building frenzy—planning public schools, universities, hospitals, roads, steel mills, airports, and whatnot. You name it, somebody had a plan to build it. Freighters loaded with cement were famously so backed up waiting to unload at the country's main port that several were drenched by repeated heavy rains, absorbed too much moisture, and sank. The capital of Lagos became the most expensive and fastest growing city in the world. Even with petrodollars flowing into the country, the government strained to keep up with the rate of urban growth in Lagos and elsewhere.

Booms of such intensity, however, are often not good things in the long run. Oil production is particularly tricky because it is capital and technology intensive. That is, the learning curve of how to extract (and refine) oil is rather steep and doing so is never cheap. And yet oil extraction employs a relatively small number of people. As a result, most of Nigeria's production (as in most other oil-producing states) was left in the hands of foreign corporations who paid significant leases directly to the Nigerian government, as well as sharing the profits from oil exports. With once-inconceivable quantities of wealth suddenly flowing through the economy, greed and corruption also blossomed. Government payrolls expanded dramatically; sometimes to fill legitimate positions, but all too often simply as politicians created positions for clients and family members as forms of patronage. Millions of dollars were diverted from public projects to private bank accounts.

Another significant side effect of the Nigerian oil boom was that other elements of the economy were abandoned. Why try to earn one's living earning peanuts by growing peanuts (during a drought, no less) when gaining access to the flow of petrodollars seemed so easy?[10] Even if one couldn't get a political position, perhaps one could gain an import license for color televisions to sell to people with oil dollars? Or perhaps there was work to be found as a driver for somebody with a brand-new Mercedes or as a cook for someone who just built a new house? Populations flocked to Nigeria's exploding cities in search of new opportunities. The result, however, was that Nigeria's economy became focused more and more on oil alone. This approach worked well enough as oil prices continued to soar over the course of the 1970s. However, in the early 1980s these prices suddenly plummeted as internal rivalries undermined OPEC's cooperation and global production began to outpace demand. Nigeria and other oil producers faced abruptly declining revenues with few other sources of national income to cushion the blow. By 1989, the value of the naira had dropped from two dollars to the naira to seven naira to the dollar. By 1992 it was thirty naira to the dollar. By 1993 it was 120 naira to the dollar. Worse, Nigeria's political class seemed unable to wean themselves from the spending habits engendered by easy oil money. Indeed, by the nadir of the 1990s, even "spigot economies" such as Nigeria's were suffering from debt crises not unlike that of their oil-poor neighbors.

---

[10] Prior to the 1970s, Nigeria was the world's largest peanut producer.

THE NEOLIBERAL TURN:
STRUCTURAL ADJUSTMENT IN THE 1980s

By the mid-1980s there was talk of a global debt crisis. Worst hit were countries such as Mexico and Brazil, which were on the verge of defaulting on their massive debt burdens. Although not quite so heavily indebted in terms of the total amount owed, most African countries nonetheless faced unsustainable "balance of payment" challenges—which simply meant that there was no way that countries could continue to make debt payments and also meet the demands for imports and maintain social services. In 1987 the World Bank estimated that debt payments equaled roughly 31 percent of total African export earnings. Loans, which had been relatively easy to come by for decades, became difficult for developing countries to acquire.

This crisis, along with a shift in the political climate that featured the rise of Reaganism and Thatcherism in the West and *perestroika* (rebuilding) in the Soviet Union, saw a gradual shift away from notions of state-centered development that had characterized so much of the twentieth century and the rise of what is often dubbed "Neoliberalism." In particular, the International Monetary Fund (IMF) and World Bank began to attach lengthy lists of conditions known as structural adjustment programs (SAPs) to desperately needed loans. Core conditions generally included a reduction of state involvement in development programs, the privatization of state-run enterprises, the opening of national economies to international investment, cutbacks in state programs such as health care and education, and an end to price controls and the fixing of the value of national currencies. At the broadest level, these mandates sought to cut the cost of government in developing economies, facilitate exports, and encourage both internal and external private investments. The trend toward distrust of government-directed development led to a growing role for what are called nongovernmental organizations (NGOs). Although these organizations could be local, many were international (INGOs). As a result, international development organizations often gained access to considerable sums of development aid and came to wield considerable influence in many African countries. Similarly, in many regions religious organizations (mostly Christian and Muslim) stepped in to provide services no longer available from (secular) governments.

The ramifications of this shift in the development paradigm were many. Although recognizing that the state-centered paradigm of development had largely failed to "deliver the goods" in the underdeveloped world, structural adjustment also brought serious complications. First, it meant a significant erosion of the sovereignty of independent states, as the leverage of debt was used to mandate a host of economic and social policies. For countries where colonialism was still fresh in people's memories, the idea of relinquishing power to the IMF and allowing foreign countries access to the economy on favorable terms was often repugnant. Further, these conditions demanded cuts in some of the areas where African states had been most successful—in particular in the provision of medical and educational services to their populations. Finally, the loosening of currency controls generally meant a rapid devaluing of state currencies and resulted in significant increases in the price of imported goods, including staple foods such as grains. These cost increases resulted in significant popular hardship and discontent. Notably, cuts in social services and government wages threatened to undermine already shaky popular support for many political regimes, a topic that will be addressed in more detail in the next chapter.

Interestingly, it was Ghana that provided one of the first test cases for the efficacy of structural adjustment in Africa. By 1980 Ghana was an economic basket case. Average per capita income had dropped by roughly 80 percent over the 1970s, industrial and agricultural production had dropped considerably, and the country was importing nearly a third of its foodstuffs. Fuel costs and debt service consumed more than half of the national budget. Under the leadership of Jerry Rawlings, who had twice come to power in military coups (most recently in 1981), Ghana established the Economic Recovery Program in close cooperation with the IMF. As a result, the government reopened the country's mining sector to foreign investment, devalued the cedi, and dropped price controls on cocoa. Although these policies brought significant hardship to the population through increased consumer prices and reduction in services, they also fostered a rapid turnaround in the Ghanaian economy, which posted growth rates averaging 5.5 percent per year through the balance of the 1980s and into the early 1990s. Ghana reclaimed its status as a major cocoa and gold exporter, for example, and also began to develop a thriving tourist industry—catering in particular to members of the African Diaspora from the Americas. Indeed, the revival of the Ghanaian economy heralded a coming turnaround in African fortunes that would begin to sweep the continent in the coming millennium.

CONCLUSIONS: BETTING ON DEVELOPMENT

The fates of African economies in the latter twentieth century tells us much about the challenge of seeking development. Even when the best advice of development experts (be they structuralists or neoliberals) is followed, the outcomes are not always predictable. Even the economic decision makers in the world's most wealthy and developed economies can be (and often are) caught off guard by international events, ecological challenges, and the vagaries of even their own markets. Indeed, the events of the past few years are perhaps the best way to close out this chapter. Since the "Great Recession" of 2008, the elder industrial powers of the United States and Western Europe have struggled to recover from near economic collapse. Several European states have found themselves subjected to IMF Structural Adjustment Programs as conditions for bailout loans—just as did so many African states in the 1980s. And, even in the United States, debates have raged over the balance between structuralist and neoliberal approaches to economic recovery. At the same time, a host of African states have undergone a period of unprecedented growth, with states such as Nigeria, Ghana, Ethiopia, and Uganda posting some of the fastest rates of economic expansion in the world over the past ten years. This is something that very few economists would have predicted only thirty years ago. But, hey, they didn't see the rise of communist China as a global economic and manufacturing powerhouse, either.

The case of Ghana and the Côte d'Ivoire is also apropos of the conclusion of this chapter. Although the Côte d'Ivoire was the hands-down winner of Houphouët-Boigny's and Nkrumah's bet in 1967, an examination of the state of the two countries' economies now suggests that perhaps Ghana has been more successful in the long run. Although Ghana struggled through the 1970s and 1980s, its economy has not only grown but also diversified significantly in the past two decades. Some 50 percent of Ghanaians work in service industries, some 22 percent in agriculture, and the remaining 28 percent are employed in industries. Conversely, some 68 percent of the Côte d'Ivoire's population continues to be employed in agriculture. Further, the country has in the past two decades been riven by civil war fueled in part by labor migration—leading to a mass exodus of French bureaucrats and investors. As of 2013, the GDP of Ghana was estimated at around $39 billion compared with about $24 billion for the Côte d'Ivoire. Similarly, the per capita income of Ghana was about $3400, with Ivorians earning only about $1400 per year. Does this mean that Ghana was actually correct to try and change the course of its economy early on and lay the foundation for greater economic diversity and independence, even if was to stumble significantly en route? Or perhaps the Côte d'Ivoire is in the midst of its own "stumble" and will soon begin to recover? Currently, the country is projected to post a staggering growth rate of 14 percent for 2013, whereas the Ghanaian economy is projected to grow at 8 percent. The point here is that the case of Africa in the latter twentieth century highlights that economic development is a terribly difficult thing to predict, and that investment, whether by the state or private capital, is always a gamble with outcomes that are all too often unforeseen.

REFERENCES AND FURTHER READINGS

Bloom, Peter J., Stephan F. Miescher, and Takyiwaa Manuh, Eds. *Modernization as Spectacle in Africa* (Bloomington, IN: Indiana University Press, 2014).

Iliffe, John. *A Modern History of Tanganyika* (Cambridge, UK: Cambridge University Press, 1979).

Mkandawire, Thandika. *Our Continent Our Future: African Perspectives on Structural Adjustment* (Dakar, Senegal: Codesria, 1991).

Minogue, Martin and Judith Molloy, Eds. *African Aims and Attitudes: Selected Documents* (Cambridge, UK: Cambridge University Press, 1974).

Peet, Richard and Elaine Hartwick. *Theories of Development: Contentions, Arguments, Alternatives* (New York: Guilford Press, 2009).

Rist, Gilbert. *The History of Development: From Western Origins to Global Faith* (London: Zed Books, 2008).

Rodney, Walter. *How Europe Underdeveloped Africa* (Baltimore, MD: Black Classic Press, 2011).

Stamp, Dudley L. and W. T. W. Morgan. *Africa: A Study in Tropical Development* (New York: Wiley, 1972).

3

A Tropical Cold War

On February 13, 1960, a nuclear bomb was detonated in southern Algeria. Code named *Gerboise bleue* (Blue Desert Rat), it was three times as powerful as the bomb dropped on Nagasaki and was the first of seventeen French nuclear tests undertaken in Algeria. Such tests were part and parcel of the Cold War's arms race, and de Gaulle enthusiastically declared "Hurray for France! This morning she is stronger and prouder!" The response to the tests in Algeria and elsewhere in Africa was far more critical. In Algeria, where partisans were waging a brutal struggle with the French for independence, the tests were seen as both an attack and a further disgrace at the hands of French colonialism. Protests against the tests had taken place across West Africa for over a year in advance of the first detonation. In 1959, the front page of Ghana's *Daily Graphic* newspaper featured a banner headline: "GHANA APPEALS TO THE WORLD: DISSUADE FRANCE FROM ATOM TESTS" (see Fig. 3.1).[1] The story went on to accuse the French of showing disregard for the possible health risks to African populations caused by the fallout that would be carried southward by the prevailing seasonal winds.

---

[1] "GHANA APPEALS TO THE WORLD," *Daily Graphic*, September 30, 1959, p. 1.

Ghana appeals to the world:

'DISSUADE FRANCE FROM ATOM TESTS'

'UK statement embarrassing'

GHANA has called upon the nations of the world to do everything in their power to dissuade France from testing atomic bombs in the Sahara.

In a statement issued yesterday, the Government said that the proposed tests would strain further the relationship between Africa and Europe.

The Government said that recent statements by Britain seeking to assure Nigeria and Sierra Leone that the tests would not endanger health in the two countries had placed "Ghana, as a member of the Commonwealth, in a most embarrassing position."

Genuine doubts

It went on: "In Africa these statements of the British Government will undoubtedly be interpreted as support for the French Government's decision and the establishment of Anglo-Nigerian monitoring stations can only underline the genuine doubts and fears which are held about fallout, even among distinguished scientists.

The Government described France's proposal as a cynical disregard for the well-being of Africans generally, especially those living in West Africa, and gave the assurance that it would not cease to protest against the contamination of the African continent.

● The sixth General Assembly of the World Federation of Scientific Workers at Warsaw, Poland, has expressed "grave concern" about the proposed tests.

In a resolution the scientists said: "Such an explosion could have incalculable political consequences".

The Assembly was attended by about 100 scientists from Communist and non-Communist countries.

OTUMFUO'S DELEGATE

Otumfuo the Asantehene has deputed Nana Boakye Dankwa, Akyempimhene, to represent him and the Ashanti Regional House of Chiefs at the funeral of Mr George Padmore, African Affairs Adviser to the Premier, which will be held in Accra on Sunday. The ashes of Padmore will be flown from Britain today.

Driver's mate is remanded

An Nsawam driver's mate, Amas Jobo, was remanded in custody for a week after he had pleaded guilty at the Nsawam Magistrate's Court yesterday to charges of possessing a pound counterfeit note and uttering a counterfeit note.

FIGURE 3.1   Atom Tests Headline from the *Daily Graphic*

The case of the Algerian nuclear tests highlights an important fact. While many histories of the Cold War focus on the ideological tensions between the United States and the Soviet Union and such confrontations as the Cuban Missile Crisis and the Vietnam War, the reality is that the Cold War also played out in significant ways in Africa. As such, this chapter seeks to highlight the interplay between the Cold War and Africa during the period up to the collapse of the Soviet Union in the early 1990s. A number of questions are addressed in the course of this chapter. How did Cold War tensions influence African decolonization and the structure and development of political systems? What sort of role did the Cold War play in facilitating or fueling tensions around the continent? Special focus is given to how Cold War's ideological tensions and involvements influenced the process of decolonization in Lusophone Africa, Rhodesia (Zimbabwe), and apartheid-era South Africa. The chapter concludes with a brief examination of how it was possible that the end to the Cold War could foster both political transformations and brutal conflicts.

IT'S AN ILL WIND—THE UPSIDE OF THE COLD WAR IN AFRICA

Although much of this chapter focuses on the negative impact of Cold War tensions and interventions in Africa, it is important to keep in mind that the ideological tussle between the capitalist and communist powers also offered a degree of political leverage to those seeking or who had recently gained independence. Just as the rise of the superpowers after World War II weakened the ability of states such as Britain and France to maintain their colonial empires, the contest among the United States, the Soviet Union, and, to a lesser extent, the People's Republic of China (PRC) for allies and client states offered African leaders and activists opportunities and options that simply had not existed a decade or two before. For example, in the first few years after seizing power in Egypt, the Nasser regime was able to garner aid from both the United States and the Soviet Union as the two superpowers courted influence in this strategically and politically significant state. Eventually Egypt opted to align itself more closely with the Soviet Union, but even that came after years of diplomatic wrangling on the part of the United States.

Another example of the Cold War creating "options" for new African states was that of Guinea. As we saw in Chapter 1, Guinea was the only French African colony to vote *non* in the 1958 referendum regarding continued economic and political relations with France. France's harsh response to Guinea's demand for full independence without strings attached was intended to make an example for other decolonizing states. However, superpower competition for client states meant that Guinea was not without potential supporters. With the French out, the new Guinean leader, Ahmed Sékou Touré, was promptly invited to make a state visit to the Soviet Union. Soon afterward, the Soviets extended considerable loans to Guinea and provided technical assistance to repair the transportation and communication infrastructure sabotaged by the French as they exited the country. Guinea also signed a military cooperation treaty with an eye toward training an officer corps to replace the French personnel who left in the aftermath of the *non* vote. In 1961 the Soviets awarded Touré the Lenin Peace Prize for the promotion of peace among nations. By and large, in the first years of independence, Guinea sought to establish a socialist economy, and the Soviet Union became a major market for Guinean agricultural and mineral exports.

Yet Touré did not simply become a Soviet client or pawn. Despite the apparent alignment with the Eastern Block, Touré remained open to improved relations with the United States, while remaining critical of US support of the apartheid regime in South Africa. Touré responded positively to President Kennedy's overtures. From 1960 to 1963 Guinea accepted aid from the US Food for Peace Program, and during the Cuban Missile Crisis he refused Soviet access to Guinean airfields. Touré also made overtures to Maoist China. Although such diplomatic shifts were of considerable frustration to the United States and the Soviet Union and resulted in frequent diplomatic condemnations, it meant that the superpowers continued to offer support in hopes of solidifying Guinea's status as a client state.

Across the continent, African leaders sought, like Touré, to take advantage of Cold War rivalries to strike trade, developmental, military, and educational deals that could be of advantage to their newly established states. In many instances, they were successful. Thousands of Africa's most promising students were provided with scholarships to study in the United States, the Soviet Union, former colonial states, and China. Loans were provided at rock-bottom interest rates, providing governments with the funds that often were believed essential (as we saw in Chapter 2) to "launch" economic growth. For example, Egypt successfully played off the United States and the United Kingdom against the Soviet Union in a bidding war to provide funds for the construction of the Aswan High Dam. In the end, the Soviets provided over one billion dollars in loans at an interest rate of roughly 2 percent. This deal marked the beginning of a close relationship between Egypt and the Soviet Union that lasted until the Camp David Accords (which came with billions of dollars of US aid) of 1979 tilted Egypt toward the United States. In the 1970s, Tanzania struck a deal with China to build the Tazara railway, linking the Tanzanian coast with the copper mines of Zambia. The project was completed in only five years (two years

FIGURE 3.2 Handover of Tazara Railway (1976)

ahead of schedule) in a cooperative effort by Chinese, Tanzanian, and Zambian workers (see Fig. 3.2). The cost to China was roughly half a billion dollars and was China's largest international development project to date.

ONE-PARTY STATES, DICTATORSHIPS, AND MILITARY RULE—A POLITICAL NADIR IN COLD WAR AFRICA?

Perhaps one of the most contentious topics of Africa's early independence era is the fate of African democracies. At independence, almost every African state was democratic in design, but within only a few short years, most had become notably undemocratic in either form or practice. Journalistic accounts of this transformation have tended to be particularly harsh. Writing in 2005, for example, Martin Meredith described the Africa's postcolonial political landscape:

> Africa, by the end of the 1980s, was renowned for its Big Men, dictators who strut-
> ted the stage, tolerating neither opposition nor dissent, rigging elections, emascu-
> lating the courts, cowing the press, stifling the universities, demanding abject
> servility and making themselves exceedingly rich ... not a single African Head of

State in three decades had allowed himself to be voted out of office. Of some 150 heads of state who had trodden the African stage, only six had voluntarily relinquished power.[2]

Although Meredith's description is inarguable at certain levels, it fails nonetheless to engage the complexity of just what internal debates and external forces had to take place in order for such sweeping changes to take place. Indeed, the fact almost every single African political system was quickly transformed from democratic to autocratic seems to suggest that there is more going on that simply the vagaries of "strutting Big Men."[3] Moreover, the fact that one-party states, military dictatorships, and assorted forms of autocracy were common not just in Africa but around the world during the era of the Cold War certainly hints that wider and more powerful forces were at work.

First, it is important to note that in many cases the democratic systems bequeathed to new African states were deeply flawed. Often, departing colonial powers sought to rig the system to ensure that certain groups or actors gained power. A case in point would be the British design of a Federal system for Nigeria that guaranteed the (initial) dominance of aristocratic Muslim rulers in the country's Northern Region and the marginalization of more nationalist leaders such as Aminu Kano or Nnamdi Azikiwe. Elsewhere, such as in the Belgian Congo, the transfer of power was so mismanaged that there was no way it wasn't going to immediately fall apart (see Fig. 3.3).

A common argument for the transformation of African political systems was the idea that multiparty democracy was poorly suited and even threatening to the needs of new African states. Numerous politicians and scholars argued that multiparty systems encouraged what was often described as "tribalism." That is, they argued that in a multiparty setting, people would not organize and vote according to ideological divisions, but rather would form political parties based on ethnic affiliations. Given that new African states generally lacked any sort of historic or national identity and were more often defined by ethnic and cultural diversity than the relative homogeneity that characterized many Western nations, the idea of reinforcing and

---

[2] Meredith, 2005, pp. 378–379.
[3] If you want to impress your instructor, now would be a good time to ask about how journalists tend to both genderize and sexualize their representations of African politics.

FIGURE 3.3   Lumumba Requiem in Cairo

giving voice to "subnational" identities through political parties was antithetical to the nation-building aspirations of many new leaders. As such, many African leaders first argued against and then moved to dismantle multiparty systems, often advocating "one-party states" in their place. Writing for the journal *Foreign Affairs* in 1963, Kenya's Tom Mboya outlined the case for the one-party state, adding that in Kenya multiparty democracy served the needs of the white minority and former colonial power more than it did the need so of the Kenyan nation:

> The Kenya African National Union (KANU) was created as soon as Africans were permitted to form national political organizations. The Kenya African Democratic Union (KADU) followed three months later, but it had no separate program and found it difficult to justify its existence until somebody's brain wave came up with the platform of "Regionalism." This fitted in with the traditional regard shown by British politicians and the press for the interests of the so-called downtrodden minority tribes or communities. A great deal of political confusion and weakness in dependent countries has resulted from this sort of practice.[4]

Tanzania's Julius Nyerere voiced similar concerns during the same year, stressing that because Tanzania had unified to overcome colonialism, no internal divisions existed to be represented by multiple parties:

> Now that colonialists have gone, there is no remaining division between 'rulers' and 'ruled'; no monopoly of political power by any section or group which could give rise to conflicting parties. There can, therefore, be only one reason for the formation of such parties in a country like ours - the desire to imitate the political structure of a totally dissimilar society.[5]

Of course, not all politicians or groups within new African states accepted the argument for the utility of the one-party state. In Ghana, the United Party and National Liberation Movement parties, which included much of the leadership of the United Gold Coast Convention (UGCC), which had begun the postwar push for greater sovereignty, found themselves opposed to many of the policies of Nkrumah and the Convention People's Party (CPP). Following an alleged attempted coup in 1958 (only one year after gaining independence), the CPP-dominated government passed a sweeping Preventive Detention Act (PDA) that allowed the government to incarcerate those accused of terrorism or sedition without trial. In one case, four members of the "Star Rockets" band were arrested and sentenced to three months hard labor for allegedly singing a song mocking Nkrumah.[6] Highlighting the Cold War

---

[4] Mboya, 1963, p. 661.
[5] "We can't import any ideas—Nyerere" *Daily Graphic*, April 16, 1963, p. 3.
[6] "Four Bandsman Sent to Jail," *Daily Graphic*, May 13, 1960, p. 9.

tensions that often influenced domestic politics during the era, the United Party issued the following statement:

> The mass arrests are a further step in the calculated establishment of a one-party totalitarian state in Ghana by the familiar Communist techniques of inventing and planting plots on leaders of the opposition party so as to effect their arrests or liquidation.[7]

Not all of the tactics used to consolidate power were judicial or violent. Often, opposition politicians were "co-opted" by means of the provision of government positions and high salaries. Whatever the case, within years of independence, effective institutional opposition had ceased in many African states. Opposition politicians were sometimes driven underground or into exile. Many leaders took the concentration of power a step further and constructed significant cults of personality as well. In Ghana, Kwame Nkrumah became known as *Osagyefo* (Redeemer) and his birthday was celebrated as "Founders Day"—a national holiday dedicated to celebrating the leadership of Nkrumah. Witness the following editorial by K. Appiah Thompson celebrating his birthday in 1965:

> Fifty-six years ago today, Osagyefo Dr. Kwame Nkrumah, one of the greatest sons of Africa in chequered history, was born. . . . Unlike some great men, Kwame was born unsung. There were no Angels to herald his birth. There is nothing on record that a peculiar star appeared in the sky. But he was destined to be the liberator of his people from abominable foreign domination. . . . Ghanaians have great cause, therefore, to crown him with the appellation of Osagyefo which is prefixed to his name. Every year at this time, all Ghanaians at home and abroad turn out to do honour to their liberator and leader.[8]

Across the country, celebrations were held and companies and government ministries took out pages and pages of adds in the newspapers congratulating *Osagyefo* on his birthday and achievements.

The concentration of power in the hands of a political leader, party, or both, was not the only challenge facing the new African polities. Across the continent (and, as already noted, around the world) military

---

7 "U.P statement on arrests," *Daily Graphic*, November 12, 1958, p. 16.

8 Thompson, K. Appiah, "SHOW LOVE BY DEEDS, Chant of 'Hosanna' is not sufficient," *Daily Graphic*, September 21, 1965, p. 5.

leaders overthrew civilian governments and placed themselves in power. Military coups often shared a common set of justifications. The civilian government was declared to have failed because of mismanagement, ethnic favoritism, and corruption. Conversely, the military, which was defined by its discipline and selfless devotion to the country, was presented as ideally suited to setting the country back on the path to freedom and development. In this vein, it was the Free Officers Movement that overthrew the Egyptian monarchy and brought Nasser to power in 1952. In 1958 in Sudan, Abdallah Khalil overthrew the government for which he served as prime minister and installed himself as the head of a military junta. He was, in turn, promptly overthrown by another Sudanese military commander, Ibrahim Abboud, who established a Supreme Council and titled himself the "Chief of the Military Government." In Nigeria on January 15, 1966, a coup led by officers from the country's predominantly Igbo southeastern region overthrew the multiparty federal government. The coup organizers assassinated many of the political leaders and military officers from the northern and western regions of the country, but not from the southeast. Upon seizing power, they justified their actions as follows (the announcement has been edited for brevity):

> In the name of the Supreme Council of the Revolution of the Nigerian Armed Forces, I declare martial law over the Northern Provinces of Nigeria. The Constitution is suspended and the regional government and elected assemblies are hereby dissolved. All political, cultural, tribal and trade union activities, together with all demonstrations and unauthorized gatherings, excluding religious worship, are banned until further notice. The aim of the Revolutionary Council is to establish a strong united and prosperous nation, free from corruption and internal strife. Our method of achieving this is strictly military but we have no doubt that every Nigerian will give us maximum cooperation by assisting the regime and not disturbing the peace during the slight changes that are taking place....
>
> You are hereby warned that looting, arson, homosexuality, rape, embezzlement, bribery or corruption, obstruction of the revolution, sabotage, subversion, false alarms and assistance to foreign invaders, are all offences punishable by death sentence.... Demonstrations and unauthorised assembly, non-cooperation with revolutionary troops are punishable in grave manner up to death.... Wavering or sitting on the fence and failing to declare open loyalty with the revolution will be regarded as an act of hostility punishable by any sentence deemed suitable by the local military commander.... Like good soldiers we are not promising anything miraculous or spectacular. But what we do promise every law abiding citizen is freedom from fear and all forms of oppression, freedom from general inefficiency

and freedom to live and strive in every field of human endeavor, both nationally and internationally. We promise that you will no more be ashamed to say that you are a Nigerian.[9]

Power within the new military government soon shifted from the coup plotters to Major General Aguiyi-Ironsi, also an Igbo. Aguiyi-Ironsi was killed in July 1966 during a countercoup led by northern military officers. A standoff ensued between the military administrations of the southeast and the other regions, and violence directed at Igbos resident in the Nigeria's north and west was common, eventually resulting in the flight of Igbo refugees and the secession of the southeast as the nation of Biafra. The Nigerian Civil War raged from 1967 to 1969, resulting in over one million casualties, most of whom were civilians in the southeast who died of starvation.

Perhaps no military coup was more deeply symbolic than the one that unseated Kwame Nkrumah on February 24, 1966, while he was on a diplomatic visit to North Vietnam and China. In less than a decade, Nkrumah had gone from the leader of sub-Saharan Africa's first independent state and the leading voice for Pan-Africanism to an exile in nearby Guinea. In Ghana, crowds flooded the streets to celebrate Nkrumah's downfall. Statues were pulled down, and the *Daily Graphic* newspaper, which had spent years declaring the greatness of *Osagyefo* declared "KWAME'S MYTH IS BROKEN."[10] Nkrumah's downfall was in part a result of his internal policies, including the repression of dissent, economic decline, and significant neglect of the military. The outlawing of all parties other than the CPP and the declaration of himself as "president for life" in 1964 probably had something to do with it, too. There were also significant international factors behind the coup. On the one hand, the coup plotters were provided with bases and resources by none other than Nkrumah's ideological rival and neighbor Félix Houphouët-Boigny.[11] Moreover, declassified documents now show that both the British and US governments knew of the plans for the coup and supported the overthrow of Nkrumah. For the United States this was because of Nkrumah's growing diplomatic ties with communist

---

[9] *Vanguard*, September 30, 2010, reprint of radio broadcast by Major Chukwuma Kaduna Nzeogwu, January 15, 1966.

[10] "KWAME'S MYTH IS BROKEN," *Daily Graphic*, February 25, 1966, p. 1.

[11] You might recall the famous bet between Nkrumah and Houphouët-Boigny from 1957. In this regard, helping to sponsor a military coup against the person with whom you have a bet is probably cheating.

states. For the British, Nkrumah's vociferous condemnation of the failure of the British to rein in the white population of Rhodesia (as subsequently discussed) and his breaking of diplomatic ties with Britain as a result were major contributing factors.

Numerous other military takeovers in Africa had strong international components. Because it maintained a significant military presence in most former colonies, France was able to choose to intervene or sit on the sidelines during coup attempts. For example, the French tacitly supported the 1966 coup that brought Jean-Bédel Bokassa to power in the Central African Republic. This was in part because Bokassa was a decorated French veteran whom de Gaulle declared "a brother in arms." Bokassa would eventually become a close friend and associate of French President Giscard d'Estaing. In 1977 the French bankrolled the $25 million ceremony in which Bokassa enthroned himself as "Emperor of Central Africa." By 1979, however, Bokassa had become a liability to the French. President Giscard d'Estaing lost his reelection bid in part because of the allegation that he had accepted substantial bribes from Bokassa while earlier serving as the French minister of finance. Eventually, Bokassa's brutal repression of his population, including an incident that resulted in the death of dozens of school children who had protested the cost of school uniforms bearing his image, resulted in Operation Barracuda, in which the French military removed Bokassa and re-installed President Dakko, whom Bokassa had initially overthrown in 1966.

Coups in Africa, 1952–1994

1952
Egypt, overthrow of monarchy.

1958
Sudan, overthrow of president.

1960
Democratic Republic of the Congo, overthrow of presidency.
Ethiopia, attempted coup against monarchy.

1961
Algeria/France, attempted coup against French president by French
    military in Algeria.

1963
Togo, overthrow and assassination of president.

1964
Gabon, attempted coup defeated with French assistance.
Sudan, coup overthrows military government.

1965
Algeria, coup overthrows presidency.
Central African Republic, coup overthrows presidency.

1966
Ghana, coup overthrows presidency.
Upper Volta, coup overthrows presidency.
Nigeria, coup overthrows prime minister.
Nigeria, countercoup overthrows military government.

1967
Ghana, attempted coup.
Sierra Leone, coup overthrows prime minister.
Togo, coup overthrows military government.

1968
Sierra Leone, countercoup returns prime minister to power.

1969
Libya, coup overthrows monarchy.
Somalia, coup following assassination of president.
Sudan, coup overthrows military government.

1971
Sudan, attempted coup by communist military faction.
Uganda, coup overthrows presidency.

1972
Ghana, coup overthrows presidency.

1974
Ethiopia, coup overthrows monarchy.

1975
Chad, coup overthrows presidency.
Comoros, coup overthrows presidency.
Nigeria, coup overthrows military government.

1976
Nigeria, failed coup results in assassination of military head of state.

1978
Somalia, failed coup attempt against military government.

1979
Central African Republic, French military operation removes head of
    state and restores previous president.
Ghana, coup overthrows military government.
Uganda, coup overthrows military government.

1980
Guinea Bissau, coup overthrows presidency.
Liberia, coup overthrows presidency.

1981
Gambia, attempted coup.
Central African Republic, overthrow of presidency.
Ghana, coup overthrows presidency.
Seychelles, attempted coup.

1982
Kenya, attempted coup.

1983
Nigeria, coup overthrows presidency.

1984
Cameroon, attempted coup.
Mauritania, coup overthrows presidency.
Guinea, coup overthrows presidency.

1985
Nigeria, coup overthrows military government.
Sudan, coup overthrows presidency.
Uganda, coup overthrows military government.

1987
Burkina Faso, coup overthrows presidency.
Tunisia, coup overthrows presidency.

1989
Ethiopia, coup attempt.

1990
Nigeria, coup attempt.

1991
Mali, coup overthrows military government.

1992
Algeria, coup results in cancellation of presidential elections.
Sierra Leone, coup overthrows military government.

1993
Nigeria, coup overthrows interim government.

1994
Gambia, coup overthrows presidency.

Another significant coup resulted in the overthrow of the Ethiopian monarch, Haile Selassie, in 1974. For decades, Selassie had served as a symbol of African independence. Yet by the early 1970s, Ethiopia (like many other African states) was facing economic and political stress. The country was battered by drought, leading to a sharp rise in food costs and regional food shortages. This hardship was compounded by the sudden rise in fuel costs resulting from the Arab Oil Embargo of 1973. Widespread protests shook Ethiopia's capital, and in 1974, Selassie was overthrown by a military coup. Known as "the Derg," the junior military officers who had orchestrated the coup declared that Ethiopia, which had been firmly in the Western Cold War camp up to that time, was now a communist state. The Derg executed numerous members of the former regime and clamped down on dissent. Rebellions broke out in many parts of the country. With Soviet aid and through the use of famine as a weapon, the new government eventually cemented its power. In the process, they sought to establish a Soviet-style command economy built around the nationalization of industry and infrastructure and the collectivization of agriculture. Civil war with Eritrean separatists and an invasion of Ethiopia's Ogaden region, which was home to many ethnic Somalis, by Somalia in 1977 brought further conflict. Notably, Somalia had been a Soviet client state since the coup of Siad Barre in 1969. Barre chaffed at the Soviet support for Ethiopia at the expense of Somali interests, and in the late 1970s opened up diplomatic ties to the United States. The United States sought to ensure its influence in the region by helping Barre to create the largest standing army in Africa.[12]

---

[12] So, if you've ever wondered how the Somalis came to have so many guns sitting around, now you know. They are a legacy of both Soviet and US support and "aid" during the Cold War.

Thus, it is important to see the famine and conflict that have plagued much of the Horn of Africa in the past forty years as not simply a result of drought, economic mismanagement, or ethnic rivalries, but also as the result of Cold War tensions and military aid that served to exacerbate and fuel those regional fires.

African leaders certainly share a responsibility in Africa's tilt toward autocracy for their desire to concentrate and hold power. However, as highlighted by the preceding discussion, it is crucial to keep in mind that the international political climate of the Cold War must also be taken into account. Indeed, it is apparent that the superpowers and the former colonial powers all found either one-party states or dictators to be easier to work with—so long as they were on "their side." Thus, the United States didn't really care if a military dictator such as Mobutu Sese Seko (the military ruler of Zaire) was notoriously brutal and corrupt—so long as Zaire could be counted on as a reliable vote in the United Nations and as a bulwark against the expansion of communism in Central Africa. Similarly, the Soviets were willing to allow the Derg to kill tens of thousands of Ethiopians by means of the manipulation of food scarcity so long as they gained an ally and foothold in the Horn of Africa. Thus, autocrats and dictators in Africa found strong allies in the superpowers during the era of the Cold War.

MINORITY RULE, THE COLD WAR, AND LIBERATION IN SOUTHERN AFRICA

Across the region of Southern Africa, local and global tensions were often even higher than those elsewhere on the continent. In South Africa, as well as in the Portuguese colonies of Angola and Mozambique, Africans faced determined resistance in the quest for sovereignty. By and large, this resistance stemmed from a complex stew of factors that involved the presence of significant immigrant European populations, many of whom adhered to ideologies that were hostile to the idea of African equality. Further, a number of strategic considerations served to amplify the role of Cold War stresses that were already implicit to the process of decolonization. For these reasons and others, the process of decolonization in Southern Africa was slower and often more violent than generally found elsewhere in the continent.

As noted in Chapter 1, the postwar era was in part defined by slow but nonetheless real progress toward inclusive political systems in many parts of the world. In the United States and elsewhere, the idea of using racial classifications to deny sovereignty gradually shifted from accepted to unacceptable for most people and governments. South Africa, however, bucked this trend. Indeed, while much of the world was working to remove barriers to multiracial political participation, South Africa was adding them. In 1948, just as India was being granted independence from colonial rule and the US military was being desegregated, the ruling Nationalist Party of South Africa implemented the system known as *apartheid*. Meaning "separation," apartheid served to build on and institutionalize a host of laws which classified and segregated South African (and Southwest African) populations on the basis of race. The Apartheid laws enacted in the late 1940s and 1950s defined the "race" of each individual based upon skin tone, hair texture, and a host of other "scientific" criteria. Marriage across racial boundaries was outlawed, as was the "Immoral Act" of sexual relations between "whites and nonwhites." More so, the Nationalist Party moved to define these categories as not only racial, but national. That is, only white people could really be South Africans. Native Africans were to be citizens of "Bantustans," which were themselves sub-categorized by "tribe." Indians and coloureds (those of mixed race) were to be segregated to specific towns or neighborhoods.

There were several complications inherent to the system of apartheid. First, whites made up only about 20 percent of the South African population, but the system defined roughly 87 percent of the country as "white lands." This meant that the Bantustans and "black townships" were, by design, overpopulated and resource poor. And yet South Africa's considerable mining, agricultural, and industrial economy depended on the low-wage labor of nonwhites. Tens of thousands also served as cooks, maids, gardeners, drivers, and the like for white families. Apartheid thus demanded that nonwhites be able to move between their segregated homelands and (white) centers of economic production. "Pass Books" and temporary labor contracts thus served as the equivalent of passports to regulate the movement of nonwhites. This system of migration not only provided white South Africans with cheap labor, but freed the government from the obligation of providing basic services or extending legal protections to those so employed.

To say that the various components of apartheid were unpopular with the nonwhite populations of South Africa and South West Africa would be a dramatic understatement. Far from isolated, those whom apartheid sought to exploit were well aware that South Africa was trying to sail into the teeth of global winds of change. In 1951, the African National Congress (ANC) and the South African Indian Congress met

to plan a Defiance Campaign in protest of the new laws and the continuing process of racial discrimination in South Africa. At the meeting,
they defined their objectives:

> All people, irrespective of the national group they belong to and irrespective of the
> colour of their skin, who have made South Africa their home, are entitled to live a
> full and free life Full democratic rights with direct say in the affairs of the govern-
> ment are the inalienable right of every South African—a right which must be
> realised now if South Africa is to be saved from social chaos and tyranny and from
> the evils arising out of the existing denial of the franchise of vast masses of the
> population on the grounds of race and colour. The struggle which the national orga-
> nizations of the non-European people are conducting is not directed against any
> race or national group. It is against the unjust laws which keep in perpetual subjec-
> tion and misery vast sections of the population. It is for the creation of conditions
> which will restore human dignity, equality and freedom to every South African.

Inspired by the process of nonviolent protest that had helped
bring independence to India just four years before, the campaign,
launched in 1952, featured boycotts, strikes, defiance of segregation
laws and curfews, and mass demonstrations in cities around the country. Part of the goal was to overwhelm the South African judicial and
penal systems as a means of highlighting the scope of discrimination
and repression in the country. The South African state was happy to
oblige, and more than 8,000 protesters were arrested during the campaign. Most received minor penalties and fines. However, the South
African government chose to pursue more serious charges against
three dozen members of the ANC's leadership. Specifically, they were
charged and convicted under the Suppression of Communism Act
that had been passed in 1950. This law and its application are significant to our understanding of decolonization in South Africa and elsewhere in the context of the Cold War on a variety of levels. First, the
law defined communism not simply as a political ideology informed
by the works of such recognized thinkers as Marx or Lenin or defined
by a particular political or economic objectives, but also as any movement ". . . which aims at bringing about any political, industrial, social
or economic change within the Union by the promotion of disturbance
or disorder, by unlawful acts or omissions or by the threat of such acts."[13]

---

[13] Suppression of Communism Act, Act #44 of 1955, Union of South Africa. Government Printer.

Thus, in the context of South Africa, simply protesting apartheid was defined as "communism."

The utility of such a definition is critical to understanding the wider context of South Africa during the Cold War. By broadly defining "communism," the South African Nationalist Party could argue that it was not repressing the rights of nonwhites, but was rather helping to combat the "global communist menace." Such a position was essential if South Africa was to maintain economic ties to and support from Britain and the United States. Further, South Africa was crucial to the United States during the Cold War in that it was the primary source of titanium, chromium, and vanadium to the NATO powers. These "strategic minerals" were so named because they were essential components of such products as jet engines and rocket motors. Without them, the United States would have been hard pressed to maintain either the arms race or the space race in which it was locked with the Soviet Union. Thus, the United States was trapped in a political catch-22 by South African apartheid. On the one hand, the US government significantly undermined its claim to democracy and racial equality by supporting the apartheid state, (especially in combination with the images of racial conflict being produced in the United States), yet it could ill afford to lose access to the region's strategic resources. Thus, by branding its opponents as "communists," the South African government was able to legitimize its actions to at least a significant number of Americans, Britons, and others.

Yet the situation in South Africa was not so simple as a repressive government cunningly discrediting its opponents by classifying them as communists. This is because there really were communists in South Africa, and they really were allied with the ANC. Indeed, several members of the ANC were also members of the South African Communist Party (SACP). Founded in 1921, the SACP had long protested racial oppression and segregation in the country. Its membership included not only blacks, but also English-speaking and Jewish South Africans. Despite being outlawed in 1950, the party's membership continued to press for an end to South Africa's rather blatant system of racial and economic oppression.

So let's take a minute to wrap our brains around the situation. Most people today agree that the apartheid regime was immoral and illegitimate, and that their willingness to use race to deny rights and quality of life to millions of people was all too harsh a reminder of the evils of fascism. Yet, most of us also agree that mid-twentieth-century communist states like the Soviet Union under Stalin or China under

Mao were far from benevolent, given their penchant for doing things like starving populations into submission and using mass incarceration to repress even mild forms of dissent. Such a situation complicates the common desire to assign clear boundaries between do-gooders and evil-doers in history. The key here, perhaps, is to note that the SACP and its allies in the ANC didn't repress much of anybody. Instead, they asked for the sort of racial justice that we today take for granted. Conversely, the South African government most certainly did repress and brutalize an awful lot of people—indeed, they repressed the vast majority of the country's population. As such, the case of South Africa and apartheid during the Cold War helps to complicate and confound some of our more simplistic characterizations of twentieth-century history.

The conflict over apartheid continued over the course of the Cold War. Crucial events included the declaration of the Freedom Charter in 1955. Core issues addressed in the Charter included universal suffrage and nationalization of land, mines, and banks. In response to the Charter, the South African government arrested many of the leaders of the ANC and charged them with treason. Following a four-year trial, all were acquitted. Clearly, the South African state had little interest in sharing power with the country's majority. Witness the following statement in the South African Parliament by Hans Strijdom, a Nationalist Party member of Parliament, in 1956:

> Either the white man dominates or the black man takes over. The only way the Europeans can maintain supremacy is by domination. . . . And the only way they can maintain domination is by withholding the vote from non-Europeans.

In the face of such ongoing institutionalized repression, many South Africans began to lose faith in nonviolent protest. In 1959 the Pan-African Congress (PAC) broke with the ANC over the issues of nonviolence and partnership with more progressive whites. In 1960, the PAC launched a series of mass protests against apartheid and the Pass Laws. At one protest in Sharpsville, South African police opened fire on the unarmed crowd, killing 69 (including women and children) and injuring 180 more. Dubbed the "Sharpsville Massacre," the event spawned even more protests, to which the South African government responded by arresting nearly 20,000 people and banning both the PAC and ANC. With organized and institutional resistance thus banned, both the PAC and ANC chose to change tactics and pursue a path of armed resistance to apartheid.

As a result, members of the ANC, including Frene Ginwala and Oliver Tambo undertook secret trips outside of South Africa to nego-tiated with Tanzania for support in establishing camps to train others to fight against apartheid. Part of the funding and staff for the camps was eventually provided by the Soviet Union, though much of it came from the Organization of African Unity's Liberation Committee. Later, some volunteers traveled from Tanzania to the Soviet Union, Eastern Block, and China for training. Perhaps the most famous of the revolutionaries to be trained in Tanzania was Nelson Mandela. Mandela had recently been exonerated of treason charges at the end of a four-year trial in South Africa. Fearing re-arrest, and having become disil-lusioned with the ability to achieve any progress through nonviolent means, Mandela went to Tanzania to receive military training. Returning to South Africa, he was arrested in August of 1962. At first charged with leaving the country illegally and fomenting strikes, he was sentenced to five years in prison. However, with the discovery of plans and materials for sabotage at an ANC hideout in Rivona, Mandela, along with eight other ANC leaders, was sentenced to life in prison. Between the crackdown after the Sharpsville Massacre and the arrest of many ANC leaders, the antiapartheid movement was largely sup-pressed for the next several years.

But while the antiapartheid movement was in a lull, in the Luso-phone colonies of Angola and Mozambique, and also in Guinea-Bissau in West Africa, the struggle for independence was moving toward a climax. Unlike the French, British, and Belgians, the Portuguese had refused to consider independence for their African colonies even in the face of popular protests and, increasingly, armed resistance. Several fac-tors lay behind Portuguese intransigence. As one of Western Europe's poorest states, Portugal had colonies that were not only more impor-tant to the home economy, but also to Portugal's identity as a world power as well. A key policy of the Portuguese state was "Lusotropicalism," which maintained that Portugal's colonies were simply overseas prov-inces of the Portuguese state—much like France had sought to treat Algeria. Perhaps even more significant, however, was the fact that Por-tugal had been ruled by the dictator António de Oliveira Salazar since 1938. Many political scholars have characterized Salazar as a fascist. As such, Africans under Portuguese rule could hardly appeal to Portuguese notions of liberty or the irony of having fought against fascism in order to demand their independence.

In Angola, the revolution began with the founding of the People's Movement for the Liberation of Angola (*Movimento Popular de*

Libertação de Angola or MPLA) in the late 1950s. The MPLA found most of its supporters among the capital of Luanda's urban *mestizo* class, often also identified as *assimilados*—Africans who had adopted Portuguese language and culture. The movement also included a number of Portuguese communists. The group, however, was severely disrupted by the Portuguese secret police, with many members being arrested and others simply killed. Cold War tensions were soon stoked when the Soviet Union began sponsoring the MPLA with weapons and training. To complicate matters, the Chinese were also supporting a rebel group, the Union for the Total Liberation of Angola (*União Nacional para a Independência Total de Angola or* UNITA). In part, these two groups reflected the growing ideological division between the Soviets and Chinese that developed over the 1950s and 1960s. Perhaps even more surprising was the presence of a third rebel group, the National Front for the Liberation of Angola (*Frente Nacional de Libertação de Angola or* FNLA), which was supported by none other than the United States. The complication here was that Portugal was a member of NATO, so in effect the United States was supporting a rebel movement against its own Cold War ally. The fact that the FNLA and other rebel movements also received support from Algeria, Ghana, France, and Israel, among others, highlights just how mind-bending the politics of liberation could be during the Cold War. By the early 1970s, following Salazar's death, the war began to shift in favor of the rebel groups, who were soon in control of much of Angola.

In 1974 the situation took a dramatic turn when the Portuguese government was overthrown in the "Carnation Revolution" and the new Portuguese administration moved to extend independence to its colonies in Africa and elsewhere. Although an initial accord established a power-sharing system between the three rebel movements, the MPLA took advantage of its control of the capital and oil-producing region of Cabinda to declare itself the party of government—significantly increasing Soviet influence in the region. The United States thus called on the FNLA and UNITA (which had recently begun accepting aid from the United States as well as China) to advance on the capital, supported by forces from Zaire and, just to make things extra complicated, apartheid-era South Africa. The MPLA forces were rather unexpectedly reinforced by some 25,000 Cuban troops. The result was an ugly multination proxy war in Angola, which by 1976 had resulted in a decisive defeat for the FNLA, Zairian, and South African forces. UNITA forces, with continued US support, remained an effective threat to the MPLA. Jonas Savimbi, the UNITA leader, was later to be celebrated by

Ronald Reagan as a "freedom fighter"—despite his early dedication to Maoist revolution. The Angolan Civil War between the MPLA government and UNITA rebels raged without resolution through the 1980s and 1990s, resulting in the deaths of an estimated one half million Angolans. One of the most telling legacies of the futility of the war was some 100,000 land mines that were left by the various belligerents and that continue to take the lives and limbs of innocent Angolans to the present day.[14]

European populations elsewhere in Southern Africa also tried to thwart the extension of sovereignty to Africans. In 1953, the colonies of Northern Rhodesia, Southern Rhodesia, and Nyasaland created the Central African Federation in hopes of preventing the expansion of African representation that was occurring in regions such as the Gold Coast. Across all three colonies, however, there were only about 300,000 whites, as compared with roughly seven million black. By the late 1950s and early 1960s, it was clear that the British were going to proceed with decolonization in Northern Rhodesia and Nyasaland, with the two becoming independent Zambia and Malawi in 1964. White Rhodesians, however, believed that even though they comprised only about 7 percent of the region's population, they could still maintain a government built around minority privilege. As one Rhodesian politician stated, the partnership between Europeans and Africans was best compared to "The partnership between the horse and its rider."[15] As such, they quickly moved to outlaw the Zimbabwean African Peoples Union (ZAPU), led by Joshua Nkomo and Ndabaningi Sithole.[16] ZAPU responded by launching a campaign of sabotage and sending recruits abroad for training. An ideological division soon developed within the party, however, and a splinter group, under the leadership of Robert Mugabe, formed the somewhat more radical Zimbabwe African National Union (ZANU). ZAPU, which eventually garnered most of its funding from the Soviet Union, held out the hope for the creation of a multiracial democracy. ZANU, on the other hand,

---

[14] In 2008, Angola hosted the first annual "Miss Landmine" pageant to bring attention to the strength of land mine survivors and continuing threat that land mines pose to peoples in former conflict sites around the world. All of the contestants had lost limbs to land mines.

[15] Meredith, 2005, p. 79.

[16] The name Zimbabwe comes from "Great Zimbabwe," a major stone enclosure built in the region around the twelfth century as part of the capital of a powerful local state. Notably, under Rhodesian law it had been illegal to suggest that Great Zimbabwe had been constructed by Africans.

was largely funded by the Chinese and voiced the desire for the creation of an all-African Zimbabwe.

In rejection of the British declaration that there would be no independence for Rhodesia without majority rule, the white Rhodesians in 1965 issued the Unilateral Declaration of Independence (UDI), severing all political ties with Great Britain. Britain declared the move "treasonous" but stopped well short of a military response, choosing instead to impose trade sanctions and banning the importation of fuel. These sanctions were later echoed by the United Nations. Nonetheless, with the aid of Portugal, which rebranded Rhodesian products as "from Mozambique," limited aid from South Africa, trade with non-UN members such as Switzerland and West Germany, and thanks to oil imports from US-backed Iran, Rhodesia was able to avoid economic collapse.

Nonetheless, Rhodesia was something of an international pariah, with no countries willing to recognize it as a sovereign state. The result was that almost all Africans in the country accepted the fact that the only path to sovereignty would be through violence. The result is what is known to white Rhodesians as the "Bush War" and to Zimbabweans as the "Second *Chimurenga*" (rebellion). With only a small population to draw on and unable to finance a sizable mercenary army, the Rhodesian state slowly lost control over the region. The collapse of Portuguese rule in Angola and Mozambique was a major blow to Rhodesia. As the war progressed, the conflict became increasingly ugly. Rhodesian forces perpetrated brutal violence against African populations suspected of "assisting terrorists." For their own part, the Patriotic Front (the uneasy alliance between the ZANU and ZAPU forces) was also willing to target civilians, as evidenced by the downing of civilian airliners with surface-to-air missiles in 1978 and 1979. The destruction of the Rhodesian strategic petroleum reserve by ZANU fighters in 1978 made clear that the Rhodesian state was no longer able to maintain security. As a result, the Rhodesians attempted to forge an alliance with "African Moderates," and in 1979 held elections and created a new state named "Zimbabwe Rhodesia" under the leadership of Methodist Bishop Abel Muzorewa. However, neither ZANU nor ZAPU was allowed to field candidates and in turn refused to accept the results of the elections. Like Rhodesia in 1965, the new state failed to receive any international recognition. British-hosted negotiations followed, and in 1980 new elections were held, resulting in a victory for ZANU that brought Robert Mugabe to power in the new country of Zimbabwe.

The collapse of Portuguese colonialism and the state of Rhodesia signaled that the days of apartheid in South Africa were numbered. Perhaps emboldened by its successful crackdown on the ANC and PAC in the 1960s, the South African state pursued a number of policies that proved to be unbearable for the country's nonwhite majority. For example, during the 1970s nearly 3 million Africans were forcibly relocated from areas classified as "white" to the Bantustans. In 1976, the government declared that Afrikaans would become the language of instruction in all schools. Protests, mainly by high school students, erupted in the Soweto region (a "black township") of Johannesburg. A crackdown by police resulted in hundreds of students dead and perhaps over 1,000 wounded. The willingness of the students to protest is often attributed to the Black Consciousness Movement (BCM) that had been launched in the early 1970s and that had sought to inculcate pride and historical awareness among black South African youth. In response, the South African government banned the BCM and incarcerated more than 100 of its leaders. One of them, Steven Biko, died after repeated beatings and torture at the hands of South African police. These events, along with many others, sparked a growing international outcry against apartheid. Protests and demands for divestment of international investments in South Africa became common scenes on university campuses around the world. Peter Gabriel, former vocalist for the band Genesis and an international music star, penned the tune "Biko" in protest of the murder, and it became both a worldwide hit and an antiapartheid anthem. By the late 1980s, even conservative politicians in the United States and Britain were loath to speak favorably of the apartheid regime.

Even among white South Africans, attitudes were changing. An economy crippled by sanctions and divestment and a state of emergency declared in response to widespread protests in 1984 and still ongoing in 1989 drove home the fact that there could be no "normal" life under apartheid even for whites. Prime Minister P.W. Botha hoped to ease discontent by revoking some aspects of apartheid, such as laws banning interracial marriage and the pass book system. In one speech, Botha informed white South Africans that they must be ready to "adapt or die." Nelson Mandela was also moved from Robin Island to a less harsh prison on the mainland. Following Botha's resignation for health reasons in 1989, F.W. de Klerk took over the leadership of the Nationalist Party and the South African government. De Klerk moved much more decisively to undertake reform, lifting the ban on the ANC and PAC, as well as permitting elections in South-West Africa and

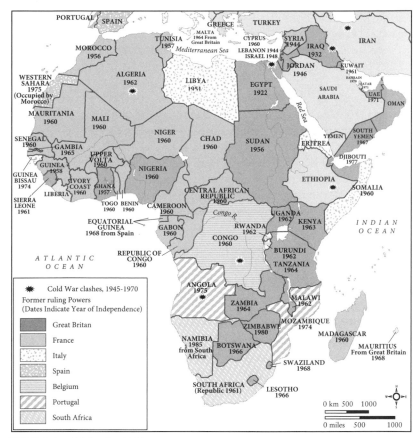

MAP 3.1   Africa in 1980

allowing the South-West African People's Organization (SWAPO) to take power in a now-independent Namibia. Perhaps most significant, de Klerk allowed the release of Nelson Mandela after some 27 years of incarceration.

South Africa began a rapid process of transforming itself from a racist minority state to a multiparty and multiracial democracy. The process was not completely without violence. Clashes between supporters of the predominantly Zulu Inkatha Freedom Party (IFP) with members of the ANC took hundreds of lives in 1992 and 1993 as party leaders maneuvered for power and local conflicts and tensions took on national significance. White extremists also sought to disrupt the move toward elections. In 1991, an armed group from the Afrikaner Resistance Movement (*Afrikaner Weerstandsbeweging* or AWB) attacked a hall where de Klerk was speaking, resulting in several deaths and injuries. In 1993, the leader of South African Communist Party, Chris Hani, was assassinated by an associate of the AWB. On another occasion, members of the AWB used an armored car to crash through the doors of and storm a building where election negotiations were being carried out. Although these events and others were certainly tragic, given the gross brutality and violence that had been perpetrated and engendered by the system of apartheid, the successful resolution of the elections, the dismantling of apartheid, and the installation of Nelson Mandela as president of South Africa in 1994 are some of the more remarkable events of the twentieth century.

CONCLUSION: AFRICA AND THE END OF THE COLD WAR

Although there was no direct connection between the destruction of the Berlin Wall in 1989 or the dissolution of the Soviet Union in 1991 and the dismantling of apartheid at roughly the same time, the parallels between the two are nonetheless apparent. Both represented political systems that had truly benefitted only a minority of those living under them and that had relied on violence and ideological contortions to survive long years of internal protest. Further, South African politicians such as de Klerk could easily see that their own strategic significance would inevitably decline with that of the Soviet Union. As such, the collapse of the Soviet Union helped deny the defenders of apartheid the utility of their claim to be fighting communism. The end of the Cold War thus helped bring about real democracy in South Africa. A similar dynamic played out on the other side of the political spectrum, as well. In 1989, Mathieu Kérékou, who had ruled Benin since 1972 as an avowed Marxist, renounced communism and agreed to a national conference on the future of the country. Once established, the delegates of the conference declared themselves the sovereign body of the state and announced that nationwide elections would be held in 1990. Kérékou was then defeated by Nicéphore Soglo and peacefully relinquished power, something very few African heads of state had done since independence. The national conference became a tool of transition to democratic elections in many countries across the continent.

Indeed, with the end of the Cold War, a host of autocrats around the world found themselves without international sponsors or ideological leverage. In some locations, such as Niger and Mali, this situation led to democratic transitions. In other countries, however, the end of Cold War patronage resulted in the collapse of states where the only source of legitimacy had been their position as superpower clients. The collapse of such rulers as Barre in Somalia, Mobutu in Zaire, and Doe in Liberia were all examples of this painful dynamic. Where once superpowers would never have allowed such total state collapse, the post–Cold War world, for all its democratic optimism, was also characterized by a painful streak of disregard as politics in Africa and elsewhere became effectively irrelevant to affairs in the industrialized world. For example, the "African Third World War" in the wake of Rwandan genocide and the collapse of Zaire has resulted in perhaps four million "unnecessary deaths" (in UN-speak) as multiple African states and local militias fought for control of this vast region's astounding mineral wealth. It is one of the more painful ironies of the twentieth century that the Cold War, which was able to bring conflict to so much of the world during its heyday, was able to bring about one final round of death and chaos in the course of its demise.

REFERENCES AND FURTHER READINGS

Armah, Ayi Kwei. *The Beautiful Ones Are Not Yet Born* (Boston: Houghton Mifflin, 1968).

Clark, Nancy and William H. Worger. *The Rise and Fall of Apartheid* (Florence, KY: Routledge, 2011).

Cooper, Frederick. *Africa Since 1940: The Past of the Present* (Cambridge, UK: Cambridge University Press, 2013).

MacKinnon, Aron. *The Making of South Africa* (Upper Saddle River, NJ: Prentice-Hall, 2012).

Mboya, Tom, "The Party System and Democracy in Africa," *Foreign Affairs*, Vol. 41, No. 4 (1963), pp. 650–658.

McMahon, Robert J., Ed. *The Cold War in the Third World* (Oxford, UK: Oxford University Press, 2013).

Meredith, Martin. *The Fate of Africa: A History of Fifty Years of Independence* (New York: Public Affairs Books, 2005).

Muehlenbeck, Philip E. *Betting on the Africans: John F. Kennedy's Courting of African Nationalist Leaders* (Oxford, UK: Oxford University Press, 2014).

Schmidt, Elizabeth. "Cold War in Guinea: The Rassemblement Démocratique Africain and the Struggle over Communism, 1950–1958," *Journal of African History*, Vol. 48, No.1 (2007), pp. 95–121.

——. *Foreign Intervention in Africa: From the Cold War to the War on Terror* (Cambridge, UK: Cambridge University Press, 2013).

Cultural Epicureanism: Music, Morality, and the African Nation

I had a band in Africa. In Northern Nigeria in the early 1990s, to be a bit more specific. Along with another grad student, we performed a mix of blues, country, reggae, and rock music. It was a great break from dissertation research, and it made us feel cool. One thing that stands out in my memory of those gigs was audience members yelling out for us to "Play Don Williams!" . . . and then looking dismayed and disappointed when we stared back blankly. The reason for this is that although Don Williams was a major country music star in the United States in the 1970s, known best for his soothing voice and tender love ballads, he was also an international smash across much of Africa (see Fig. 4.1). To this day, you can buy his music in urban and rural markets from Gambia to Botswana. Even as William's career waned in the United States, he remained popular in many parts of Africa, and he played in Zimbabwe in 1997. Our Nigerian audiences were

FIGURE 4.1   Don Williams

dumbfounded that a couple of American musicians could have no idea who someone as famous as Don Williams was.

Don Williams' African superstardom is a good way to complicate our thinking about African music in the twentieth century. When most westerners think of African music, they imagine drummers performing at some sort of exotic ceremony. Few would know that electric bands like Zimbabwe's Bhundu Boys grew up listening to Don Williams (they would later record covers of his songs, along with Johnny Cash's "Ring of Fire"). Like the continent, African music is hugely diverse. Musical styles vary significantly from region to region. In contrast to notions of Africa as a static land defined by "tradition," the music of Africa has always been changing. In some cases music changed because of local innovations, in others because of the development and introduction of new instruments or because of exchanges of styles with other African regions. And, as with Don Williams, sometimes local tastes changed because of global influences.

Although such forces have long been at play, there is no doubt that they accelerated in recent centuries, and this rate of musical exchange and development broke the sound barrier (right along with rocket and jet aircraft) during the second half of the twentieth century. This new rate of change is a result of what some call the "death of distance." This is the idea that modern technologies, including phonograph records, radio broadcasting, container ships, cell phones, and he Internet, have rendered the role of distance less and less significant shaping people's lives. Once, where you lived determined what music you could hear. Now, thanks to YouTube, iTunes, and other Internet sources, that is not the case. But even in the 1930s, it was possible to sit in a bar in Luanda, Angola, and listen to an American recording of the Cuban song "The Peanut Vendor." This song, and the thin platters of vinyl on which it traveled, helped launch a rumba craze that extended across Africa and around the world.

A Sierra Leonian lawyer, Ambrose Ganda, describes the impact of the gramophone in his youth:

> I remember as a young boy standing around the gramophone on a moonlit night. It was a tremendous novelty, and was owned by a local teacher or some big businessman. The music was mainly Sierra Leonean – songs by Ebenezer Calendar and others, in Mende. Around 1955 we started getting Zulu records. We used to have dances in the main courtyard, to music by Jean Bosco and Jim Laco. To get records, we'd make a list and someone would go to the nearest town, Bo, to buy them from an Indian shop.[1]

Although this chapter addresses how new technologies transformed African music (just as they did everywhere), it also argues that the changing political and social context of Africa in the period from 1945 to 1992 helped define these changes. In particular, this chapter emphasizes that the advent of political and cultural sovereignty that came with decolonization helped drive the process of musical development and synthesis across the continent. By choosing the instruments and music they liked, and by often transforming the roles of those instruments and by blending "outside" musical influence with local styles, musicians and audiences were in a way defining what it meant to be African citizens of the world in the latter twentieth century (see Fig. 4.2). They were, in the words of Marissa J. Moorman, practicing "cultural sovereignty." But such choices were not without controversy, and another goal of this chapter is to highlight how music also played into debates over identity, politics, and morality.

It would be impossible to cover the diversity of shifting musical styles across the continent during the time in question in a single brief chapter. As much as I would love to discuss styles such as Zam Rock (a sort of Zambian heavy metal) or the great diversity of jazz found in South Africa, this chapter examines three case studies of the development and role of just a few music styles from a few locations around the continent. These are the development and controversy over Rai in

---

[1] Quoted in Stapleton and May, 1987, p. 19.

FIGURE 4.2   "Our Own Music," from the *Daily Graphic*

Algeria from the 1940s to the 1990s, the spread of and debates concerning soul music in Tanzania in the 1960s and 1970s, and the explosion of rock, funk, and Afrobeat in Ghana and Nigeria in the 1960s through the 1980s. This chapter seeks to provide a glimpse into the diversity of ways music reflected and effected shifts in African culture and identity during an era when African states were not only gaining independence, but in a time when Cold War tensions and global youth movements often set the tone for daily life.

BACKGROUND: OF ETHNOMUSICOLOGY AND WORLD HISTORY

In 2003, Kofi Agawu, a Ghanaian-born musicologist offered the following insight:

> Why is the most widely heard music on the [African] continent not also the most
> written about, the most taught in our institutions, the most valued? The reasons
> for our reticence reside in the very circumstances in which knowledge is produced
> in Africa, in models of scholarship imported from European musicology, in the

relative lack of participation by emancipated African actors, and in the absence of methodologies suited to music that apparently falls between stools.[2]

Professor Agawu is a very smart guy. Until very recently, hardly anybody took African popular music seriously.[3] Most studies of African music were steeped in notions of "tradition" and were bounded by cultural and racial categories that were deemed to be very old, if not outright ancient. From this perspective (which also defined much of twentieth-century anthropology), things are "pure" and real only so long as they are untainted by outside influence. As a result, the goal of ethnomusicologists focusing on African music was to get at what elements were "truly African" and to highlight how African musical forms were distinct from those found elsewhere in the world. African popular music of the twentieth century, which almost inevitably embraced "foreign" influences, was deemed somehow "less African," even though it was what most Africans listened to. So, even if students in the United States or elsewhere in the world did happen to study African music, they would learn about "traditional" instruments and song structures, and no doubt how they were "embedded" in local cultural practices. For example, in the classic 1974 text *The Music of Africa*, J. H. Kwabena Nketia, another Ghanaian, states "In Akan society . . . the puberty rite for girls is celebrated by women, and the songs and drum music for this occasion are accordingly performed by adult women."(p. 36). Now, it's not that Professor Nketia was wrong about the Akan women and their drums, but this sort of exotic approach to African music leaves out a lot of the story and creates the impression that African music must be distinct from that of other parts of the world.

In recent years "The New World History" has suggested that rather than looking at people and places as distinct and seeking out differences, we might instead look for commonalities and connections between peoples. Similarly, more and more anthropologists have accepted the idea that cultures, far from being fixed and bounded, have always been changing and interacting. Looking at African popular music lets us see that it is possible for musicians and audiences to embrace and adapt "foreign" music and yet remain African. Much of

---

[2] Agawu, 2003, p. 118.
[3] There are some notable exceptions to this generalization. They include C.A. Waterman, Werner Graebner, John Collins, Gerhard Kubik and, more recently, Nathan Plageman.

the research on which this chapter is based reflects a sea change in how anthropologists and historians understand and construct culture, history, and the idea of being African. Notably, millions of Africans, through the apparently simple act of creating and listening to new styles of music, beat them to this very modern perspective by at least several decades (if not perhaps even centuries).

RAI, REVOLUTION, AND RELIGION IN ALGERIA

In Algeria, the music known as Rai has endured a host of challenges. As the scholar Marc Schade-Poulsen has observed, Rai has lain at the center of a number of Algerian debates in the past few decades:

> Low culture versus high culture, commercialism vs self-expression, poetic eloquence versus lack of proper words, vulgarity vs the family, youth versus experience, Algeria versus the West—all have been mediating words in the debate surrounding a musical form in which Algerian identity was seen to be at stake.[4]

Today, Rai is a global music. Many Rai stars now live, record, and perform in France and elsewhere in Europe. They undertake tours to countries as far-flung as the United States and India. Rai can be heard on the radio from Brazil to Australia. But although scholars generally agree that Rai as a music form probably developed first in the Mediterranean port city of Oran, exactly when Rai became Rai is not clear. This is as it should be. Musical styles do not appear out of thin air. They inevitably develop out of change. That change may be cultural, it may be technological, and it can be political as well. Like most parts of the colonized world in the twentieth century, Algeria had such change in spades, which goes a long way toward explaining why the rise of Rai has been so tumultuous. As a port, Oran had a population who interacted with peoples from around the world. Algeria was also influenced by the French, who had colonized the country after an invasion and conflict that lasted from 1840 to the 1870s. But connections with other parts of Africa, the Middle East, and Southern Europe were also important. The presence of large numbers of Axis and Allied troops during World War II introduced even more elements to the stewpot that produced Rai.

---

[4] Schade-Poulsen, 1999, p. 26.

It was during the 1950s that performers began to ider
music as "Rai," an Arabic word that roughly translates as '
ion." Male performers of Rai called themselves *Cheikhs*, which implied that the singers were old and wise. The music reflected a style of
poetic recitation and performance that had existed in the Maghreb
since the sixteenth century. But the music was open to innovation.
During the 1950s, Rai *Cheikhs* such as Bellemou Messaoud began in-
corporating "Western" instruments such as violins and accordions
into their ensembles, while also drawing on stylistic elements such as
jazz, rumba, cha-cha, and mambo. These were elements that had
been introduced by the movement of human beings, new technologies, and expanded levels of commerce. The aforementioned worldwide rumba craze of the 1940s and 1950s, for example, had helped
introduce Cuban and Latin rhythms to Algeria through the sale of
78 rpm records.

Although the *Cheikhs* and their music were generally respected
in Algerian society, the same could not be said for *Cheikhas*, who
were female performers of Rai. These women often performed with
male musicians and other female dancers, typically in bars selling
hashish, in brothels, or at the "pleasure parties" known as *bastas*.
Indeed, in a classic catch-22 of the gendering of social roles and
space, the very fact that female singers were considered risqué in
Algeria meant that they had no choice but to perform in socially mar-
ginal settings, settings that were increasingly reflected in the content
of their songs. The nature of such performances meant that the
Cheikhas were associated with alcohol, drugs, sexual license, and
prostitution. Like the *Cheikhs* of the 1950s, however, the *Cheikhas*
also incorporated new musical instruments and styles, in part because they relied on the same groups of backing musicians as did
the *Cheikhs*.

The 1950s were a time of great upheaval in Algeria. A wave of decolonization that had begun with India in 1947 was spreading across
much of the Middle East, Southeast Asia, and Africa. As we saw in
Chapter 1, Algerian nationalists rose up and fought a bloody war
against the French to gain independence. The victorious *Front de
libération nationale* (FLN) then created a one-party state that embraced socialism and Pan-Arabism. The government sought to highlight
what was "Algerian" and reject elements of Western or "imperialist"
culture. In 1964 the FLN declared that *Andalous* was to be the "National Classical Music" of Algeria. *Andalous* had originated in Muslim
Iberia centuries before and was typically performed by professionally

trained musicians of high status. Such music suited the interests of political and economic elites in independent Algeria, as did musical styles from Egypt and elsewhere in the Arab World. But Rai faced official disapproval because it was tainted by its incorporation of "Western" instruments and styles and by the social marginality of the *Cheikhas*. As a result, Rai was banned from radio broadcast (at the time, the FLN government controlled all radio and media outlets). Similarly, the government denied Rai artists the ability to record music for sale.

Yet the popularity or Rai increased. During the 1960s, Rai musicians incorporated instruments such as the trumpet, saxophone, and electric guitar and bass, which allowed them to play for larger audiences and make the music more danceable and appealing to young urban audiences. The musician Shikh Mohammad Zargui is credited with being the first to utilize an electric guitar with a wah-wah pedal (popularized in rock music by Jimi Hendrix, among others) to perform melodies previously played on reed flutes.

The popularity of Rai continued to grow through the 1970s, despite the ongoing government ban. The audience also grew more youthful. Notably, Rai was denigrated as the music of the *Hittiste* ("those who hold up the walls")—a reference to the multitudes of young unemployed men who, in a period of economic recession, spent their days leaning against the sides of buildings. By the latter 1970s a number of younger musicians embraced Rai. The new performers called themselves *Chebs* and *Chabas*, meaning "young" and "attractive," to distinguish themselves from the older *Cheikhs* and *Cheikhas*. But it was another technological innovation that was to propel the *Chebs* and *Chabas* to prominence: the cassette recorder. In the 1970s, portable cassette recorders costing around US $20–30 were developed for popular consumption. Not only could they be used to record live performances, but people could cheaply copy cassette tapes to sell or share with friends. One of the very first breakout Rai hits was "*Trigue lycee*" ("The Road to School"), recorded by the sixteen-year-old Cheb Khaled (see Fig. 4.3). Tens of thousands of cassette copies made their way across Algeria and made Khaled one of the first of a new generation of Rai superstars. Cheba Zahouania similarly became one of the dominant female performers The Baba Brothers, Rachid and Fethi, are credited with being the first to incorporate drum machines into their performances, further modernizing the sound. The *Chebs* and *Chabas* also addressed socially forbidden topics, including sex, alcohol, and poverty in a way that perhaps only the *Cheikhas* had done

FIGURE 4.3   Cheb Khaled (1989)

previously. But now the topic was moving out of the cabarets, brothels, and bars and into people's homes, transported by the new grassroots technology of the cassettes. Interestingly, the success of the new *Chebs* and *Chabas* helped open up wider audiences to the older generation of *Cheikhas*, while the *Cheikhs* remained behind. One such artist, Cheikha Remitti, saw her popularity explode in the 1980s and 1990s. Indeed, at the time of this writing, she is still a popular performer in her eighties.

Another transformation came in 1982, when a joint French and Moroccan venture established a new radio station in Tangier, Morocco, which was capable of broadcasting across much of Algeria. The station played popular Rai songs, effectively circumventing the Algerian ban on Rai. However, the Algerian government seems to have been rethinking its policy toward Rai, and they soon revoked the ban. This may have been due to the music's growing popularity with influential Algerian populations living in France and Europe. Also critical seems to have been the growth of Islamist activism in Algeria. In the 1980s, the influence of a conservative political Islam was expanding. Algerian Islamists criticized the political corruption of the FLN government and the social corruption they saw represented by Rai. Many observers thus understood the government's lifting of the ban on Rai and sponsorship of nationally televised Rai festival in 1985 as a calculated move to counter Islamist influence by encouraging the spread of Rai—an excellent example of the complex relationship among music, politics, and perceptions of morality.

In 1988, riots swept the country as popular discontent with the government and economic situation flared. Cheb Khaled's song "El Harba Wayn" ("To Flee, But Where?") became one of the anthems of the protests:

> Where has youth gone?
> Where are the brave ones?
> The rich gorge themselves.
> The poor work themselves to death.
> The Islamic charlatans show their true face.
> You can always cry or complain
> or escape . . . but where?

In response, a new constitution was authored, and in 1990 and 1991, multiparty elections were allowed for the first time since independence. A new Islamic party, the Islamic Salvation Front (*Front Islamique du Salut* or FIS), was swept into power in local elections, and one of their first moves was to ban Rai (and the sort of establishments where Rai was performed). When it appeared that the FIS would win a majority in the national elections of December 1991, the Algerian army seized power and annulled the results. The result was brutal communal conflict that pitted supporters of the secular military state against the Islamists. In the course of the conflict, Rai musicians sometimes were targeted. Cheb Hasni, called "The Prince of Rai" was shot and killed outside an Oran nightclub in 1994. Many of the more popular musicians fled to France, where their music continued to grow in popularity.

Over the course of the 1990s, the success of Rai helped propel artists such as Cheb Khaled to become not only stars of Rai but also stars of a growing genre dubbed "World Music." It is a testimony to the ability of music to flourish despite both political and religious sanctions that a music that faced almost continuous restriction in its country of origin could survive and even thrive to become global. In an interview in India in 1992, Khaled gave voice to the decline in the importance of national boundaries and cultures in influencing musical tastes: "Music has no frontiers," he said, "It belongs to the World. It belongs to the Universe."[5]

---

[5] Cheb Khaled quoted in *The Daily*, Bombay, September 27, 1992. From Marc Schade-Poulsen, "Which World: On the Diffusion of Algerian Rai to the West," in Karen Fog Olwig and Kirsten Hastrup, *Siting Culture: The Shifting Anthropological Object* (London: Routledge, 1997) p. 59.

A NATION WITHOUT SOUL?
TRADITION, MUSIC, AND IDENTITY IN
POSTINDEPENDENCE TANZANIA

As discussed in Chapter 1, in the 1960s, Tanzania was considered one of the coolest places on earth. Having achieved independence from the British in 1961, the Tanzanians, under the leadership of President Julius Nyerere, had launched a plan for economic and political development that sought to break with both European capitalism and Soviet-style communism. Nyerere declared that by building on the natural African inclination to communalism, the various ethnic groups of Tanzania could come together to build a new society based on equality, self-reliance, and cooperation. Through this "African Socialism," the new country could avoid building up debt or falling prey to Cold War political entanglements. Tanzania's initiative was a hit not only with many Tanzanians, but with Western academics and radicals. Activists and progressives from around the world, including members of the Black Panther Party from the United States, moved to Tanzania to become part of this radical experiment in nation-building and development.

Nyerere's vision for a united, prosperous, and independent Tanzania was an ambitious one. British colonialism had done little to strengthen the country's economic base, and the new state remained dependent on the export of a few cash crops for funds. British Indirect Rule had exacerbated divisions between the country's roughly 120 ethnolinguistic groups. Further, Nyerere's strong stand against apartheid and criticism of capitalism placed him in apparent opposition to "The West" in the Cold War, though his adaptive take on socialism did not put him clearly in the Soviet or Chinese camps, either.

Crucial to Nyerere's strategy of nation building in Tanzania was the idea that Tanzanian culture needed to be celebrated. He believed that African culture had been devalued by colonialism and that a renewed celebration of indigenous Tanzanian practices would help build a sense of national pride. Nyerere's focus on culture also included music. As he stated in an address to Parliament on the first anniversary of independence,

... we were taught to sing the songs of the European. How many of us were taught the songs of the Wanyamwezi or of the Wahehe? Many of us have learned to dance the "rumba," or the "chachacha," to "rock-en-roll" and to "twist" and even to dance the "waltz" and the "foxtrot." But how many of us can dance, have even heard of, the Gombe Sugu, the Mangala, the Konge, Nyang'umumi, Kiduo or Lele Mama? Most of us can play the guitar, the piano, or other European musical instruments. How many Africans in Tanganyika, particularly among the educated, can play the African drums? . . . It is hard for any man to get much real excitement from dances and music which are not in his own blood."[6]

In making this statement, Nyerere was adding his voice to a chorus of calls for what might be called "cultural nationalism" from across the continent and elsewhere in the postcolonial world. To this end, Nyerere called for the creation of a new Ministry of National Culture and Youth:

> I have done this because I believe that its culture is the spirit of any nation. A country which lacks its own culture is no more than a collection of people without the spirit which makes them a nation. . . . So I have set up this new Ministry to help us regain our pride in our own culture. I want to seek out the best of the traditions and customs of all the tribes and make them part of our national culture."[7]

It is particularly interesting that the new ministry was to focus on both "culture and youth." Although very few people would argue that the celebration of national cultural traditions is a bad idea, it is important to note that this initiative was taking place at a time when global youth culture and generational consciousness were gaining momentum. And indeed, the coming of independence meant that places like the Tanzanian capital of Dar es Salaam were becoming increasingly cosmopolitan. Connections with the wider world were becoming stronger and more numerous. Among the things coming to Tanzania by means of these newly strengthened ties with the wider world were new forms of music, as made clear by Nyerere's speech. Music came in the form of radio broadcasts. It came on LPs. It came in the soundtracks of movies that were shown in urban cinemas and from mobile movie trucks (a different sort of drive-in) in the countryside.

By the late 1960s, the cities and towns of Tanzania were home to bands that performed a dizzying array of styles. *Dansi*, which was heavily influenced by Zairian guitar-driven styles, was performed by such popular acts as the "Atomic Jazz Band." In a 1969 newspaper article about a new soul band named "Air Bantou," the *Sunday News* reporter Hadji Konde described the variety of music styles one could

---

[6] Nyerere, J. K. Tanzania National Assembly Official Reports (Dar es Salaam, 1962), p. 9. Quoted in Stapleton and May, 1987, p. 23. See also Askew, 2002, p. 13, and Ivanska, 2011, p. 37.

[7] Askew, 2002, p. 13.

hear in Dar es Salaam: "This can be soul, blues, cha-cha, samba, the latest local crazes—sukusa, kirikiri, toyota, and for good measure, the old dances like the tango."[8] The very names of the bands and song styles often reflected a sense of modern identity and global connections. The fact that a hot new Tanzanian soul band in 1969 would call itself "Air Bantou" speaks volumes about their identity as members of both modern and the global society. Soul music, popularized by James Brown and others, was particularly popular in Tanzania, which likely reflected both a sense of cosmopolitanism and the important role of Afro-American culture in defining black modernity and consciousness. Listening and dancing to soul in Tanzania was commonly referred to as "soul digging."

But the enthusiastic embrace of new and international cultural influences in Tanzania was not universal. In October of 1968, Tanzanian cities such as Dar es Salaam saw popular protests against women wearing miniskirts and pantsuits. Women so dressed found themselves harassed and sometimes assaulted on public transport and in the city streets. These attacks were soon followed by "Operation Vijana," organized by the government-supported Youth League, which sought to discourage the wearing of "indecent dress" by Tanzanian men and women. Notably, although most Western dress was considered acceptable for Tanzanian men, skirts shorter than knee length were considered "mini" for women. The campaign, which featured police raids on night clubs where trendy young women tended to congregate, brought extensive public debate. In a letter to the *Standard* newspaper, Christopher Mwesiga championed the campaign:

Thigh exposition does not only make men admire the beauty of the female sex. It also makes the observer grow sexually wild. Girls have no mercy in making people wild, and yet they do not offer satisfaction to the passions they create.[9]

A young woman, Bi. L. I. Minja, wrote a letter to *Uhuru* that aggressively identified both the generational and rural–urban tensions that were part of the debate:

The countryside and the city are not a bit alike. You elders, your time has passed, and this is our time as youth. . . . you might as well go live on the farm, plant your vegetables, and don't get hot and bothered for nothing by lovely city girls.[10]

---

[8] Ivanska, 2011, p. 72.
[9] Mwesiga, Christopher *Standard*, August 20, 1972 p. 4. From Ivanska, 2011, p. 101.
[10] From Ivanska, 2011, pp. 120–121.

Yet another ban soon followed. On November 12, 1969, a Mr. Songambele, a regional commissioner of the Tanzanian government, declared that soul music was "banned from being played in Dar es Salaam."[11] An editorial in the government newspaper, *The Nationalist* stated that soul music was

> ... a sugar-coated imperialist gimmick aimed at clouding African minds and diverting attention from the realities of life. . . . Soul music and soul digging are alien to a socialist way of life, let along socialist morality. [Soul] tries to intoxicate our youth with all the false promises in the world. Even as an instrument of self-rediscovery, soul gives us nothing more than telling us that we are black. It suggests nothing as a means towards our emancipation . . . soul is not revolutionary. Does this then not explain why the imperialists have been very keen to import this cancerous ulcer into our country?[12]

The ban brought a fresh flurry of responses:

> To me and all the teenagers this has brought a tremendous oppression which cannot be expressed. And, one unpleasant thing to note about the banning of soul is that it has reduced a great percentage of happiness to many young Tanzanians living in Dar es Salaam.—Ungando
>
> It appears to me that Mr. Songambele doesn't like Soul music. Maybe because he doesn't know how to dig it.—Maganja-Stone Chimlo
>
> Those who do not know [how] to dance and who do not keep up with the changes of life in the way of music, let them keep away from dancing places.—A. J. Kanonoi[13]

Voicing a generational identity that extended far beyond Tanzania, Charles M. Njan stated " Does this mean that our youths should not adopt any style that is liked by their co-youths on earth?"[14]

---

[11] "Songambele bans 'soul' music," *Standard*, November 13, 1969. From Ivanska, 2011, p. 69.

[12] *The Nationalist*, quoting Commissioner Songambele in "Tanzania Saves its 'Soul'" *Milwaukee Journal*, January 14, 1970. The very fact that the *Milwaukee Journal* would pick up such a story highlights the importance of the Cold War context in even Tanzanian debates over culture and identity.

[13] Quoted from Ivanska, 2011, p. 77.

[14] Letter to the *Standard*, quoted in the *Milwaukee Journal*, January 14, 1970.

Another letter, from Bob Eubanks, an African American stuuᴄ᷈ᴛ studying at the University of Dar es Salaam, is interesting in its complication of what exactly is meant by "Western":

> Soul music comes from the Blues, which is Afro-American Music. . . . Brothers and Sisters of Tanzania, do not forsake your ancestors who died in that strange and foreign land of America: and we, the Afro-Americans of today, are their children. All Power to the People. A Soul Brother.[15]

In response, *The Nationalist* published another editorial stating that

> [the ban on Soul] has brought back to the surface hitherto hidden reactionary elements within our society, disguised as 'soul diggers.' The new tactic of the imperialists is to unleash a cultural aggression through films and various types of neurotic dins, which for commercial purposes are named 'rock n roll,' 'shake,' and now 'soul.'[16]

The ban on soul was short lived. Late in 1969, a broadcast on Tanzanian government radio stated that although soul music was undesirable, the ban was impossible to enforce. The public discourse over soul and other "Western" music in Tanzania, along with other accouterments of 1960's styles of dress and dance, was nonetheless telling of a complex debate over what was a suitable investment of energy and identity for the youth of this politically radical East African state. Indeed, the contrast between the apparent political "radicalism" of Tanzania and the state's cultural conservatism highlights just how diverse political and cultural responses to the global environment of the 1960s and 1970s could be.

AFRICAN CULTURAL EPICUREANISM? POPULAR MUSIC IN NIGERIA AND GHANA

So far, we have examined settings where states sought to restrict, albeit unsuccessfully, the cultural sovereignty of the populations under their authority. It would be misleading, however, to suggest that the denial of free choice regarding music was common to African

---

[15] Letter by Bob Eubanks to the *Standard*, from Ivanska, 2011, p. 74. Also quoted in the *Milwaukee Journal*, January 14, 1970.
[16] *Nationalist* editorial, quoted in the *Milwaukee Journal*, January 14, 1970.

states and societies during the period in question. At the risk of broad generalization, it is likely that Africans have proven themselves to be some of the world's greatest "cultural epicureans"—that is, they are remarkably open minded about new and even "foreign" cultural elements. Moreover, Africans have not simply adopted new cultural elements wholesale, but have used them to create new and exciting forms of what might be called "fusion culture." Thus, while many in the twentieth century, particularly in "the West," were absorbed with the goal of organizing and bounding culture into such constructions as civilizations, races, nations, or tribes, many Africans were busily blurring the lines of such divisions even as they were created. Thus, much as the "New World History" has served to challenge the divisions between established units of geographical and cultural analysis, African cultural epicureanism has helped blur the lines between not only local ethnicities, but also such meta-notions as "African" and "Western." Perhaps nothing better represents this dynamic than the burst of musical creativity found in Ghana and Nigeria during the 1960s, 1970s, and 1980s.

As people in the first sub-Saharan country to achieve independence (in 1957), and as leading advocates of Pan-Africanism under Kwame Nkrumah, Ghanaians have a embraced a national identity of being trendsetters. Nigeria is the most populous country and has the largest economy on the continent, with a current population of roughly 170 million. Nigeria has experienced periods of "Oil Boom" and "Oil Bust" that have put Nigerian citizens on a roller coaster ride of wealth, poverty, and corruption. Yet a shared characteristic of Ghana and Nigeria is the forward-looking and optimistic nature of their populations, even in the face of considerable hardship. And perhaps this is one of the explanations for both countries' often open-minded approach to world culture—especially in those coastal regions more directly connected to the wider world via the Atlantic Ocean.

With economic connections to the wider Atlantic world stretching back to the fifteenth-century gold trade, the region of contemporary Ghana has a long tradition of music exchange. The military bands stationed at European trading posts along the Gold Coast first introduced brass instruments to the region in the sixteenth century—a technology that Ghanaians, Nigerians, and other West Africans enthusiastically embraced. In the 1960s and 1970s, almost all popular music groups in the region featured horn sections. Moreover, the forced migration of enslaved West Africans to the Americas laid the foundation for the syncretistic American, Latin, and Caribbean musical forms of jazz, blues, rumba, merengue, rock and roll, and reggae that would so influence the world in the twentieth century. Even the "country music" of Don Williams was ultimately a result of this fusion. In a perfectly chosen metaphor, the Ghanaian scholar John Collins has dubbed this cycle of influence "feedback"—highlighting the circulation of musical styles and influences back and forth across the Atlantic.

One of the most significant musical developments in twentieth-century Ghana and Nigeria was Highlife. Although the style has its origins in music developed along West Africa's Atlantic coast in the nineteenth century (and spread by Kru sailors from Sierra Leone), the term first developed in Ghana in the 1920s to describe the music performed by large bands in local clubs. Highlife grew into distinctive substyles. One style was that performed by large jazz-style bands such as the one led by E.T. Mensah, one of the founders of the genre. Louis Armstrong and his All-Stars' tour of Nigeria and Ghana in 1956 received considerable press coverage in both countries, in no small part because of the meeting of Armstrong and Mensah for a concert and jam session in Accra, Ghana. Smaller guitar-band Highlife groups were influential for their performances in smaller towns and venues. Through the close economic connections between the two regions, Highlife spread from Ghana to Nigeria in the 1940s and became hugely popular. Cross-pollination with the guitar bands and slower guitar-based music of the "Palm-Wine" style helped lead to the creation of "Juju" music in Southwestern Nigeria, particularly in Lagos. Thanks in part to the stardom of King Sunny Ade, Juju would find an international audience in Great Britain and the United States during the late 1970s and 1980s.

The 1960s and 1970s saw an explosion of Afro-rock, Afro-funk, and Afro-soul performed by dozens of Ghanaian and Nigerian groups. Nigerian bands such as "The Hykkers," "MonoMono," and "Ofo the Black Company" produced rock and roll and funk that were heavily influenced by British and American bands, yet laced with tonal variations and complex rhythms fostered by the incorporation of local musical elements. The adaptation of the electric bass to performing not only stringed parts, but to playing rhythm lines previously performed by an instrument often called a "talking drum"(because a tensioning mechanism allowed the drum's tone to be raised and lowered to mimic a human voice) added a complexity to these compositions that is hard to describe in print.[17] In the early 1970s, the Ghanaian and West

---

[17] Almost every band, performer, or song mentioned in this chapter is available for purchase online or for streaming on YouTube. Check 'em out – I bet you'll be glad you did.

Indian Band, Osibisa, scored a series of hits not only in Ghana, but also in Great Britain with songs such as "Woyaya" and "Sunshine Day," establishing themselves not only as an Afro-rock band, but also as a "progressive rock" band on par with Yes and Camel. Interestingly, as Osibisa's fame in Europe declined in the mid-1970s, many identified the cause as the fact that the band "wasn't African enough." The band's leader, Teddy Osei, replied to these charges in an interview in the British Magazine *Black Music* in 1974:

> First they said our music was not pure African stuff because we've westernized it with the addition of western instruments like the keyboards and guitars, and that we were moving away from our roots by pandering to the British progressive-rock movement. But I have always said, we live in a new environment different from what we knew [before], so our music must somehow reflect this new influence.[18]

Another representative musician was the Nigerian artist William Onyeabor, who graces the cover of this book and sold tens of thousands of albums in Nigeria.[19] Onyeabor was notable first for his embrace of new technologies, producing complex layerings of synthesizers, drums, and bass in his own twenty-four-track studio. Educated both in Nigeria and the Soviet Union (where he studied cinematography), Onyeabor also brought global topics and consciousness to his compositions. His hit song "Better Change Your Mind," released in 1978, offered the following commentary on the Cold War, global power, and racial identity:

> America, do you ever think this world is yours? Eh?
> And you Russia, do you ever think this world is yours?
> You China, do you ever think this world is yours? Eh?
> And you Cuba, do you ever think this world is yours?
> Canada, do you think this world is yours? Eh?
> And you Britain, do you think this world is yours?
> If you're thinking so, my friends . . .
> Better change your mind.
> Because there is no other one, except God, who owns this world.

---

[18] Teddy Osei, interview by Bob Okenodo, "The Magnifunk Seven," *Black Music*, December, 1974, pp. 22–23, in Stapleton and May, 1987, p. 76.
[19] In 2013, the record label Luaka Bop would rerelease a number of William Onyeabor's songs as an album titled "Who is William Onyeabor?"

Front man, do you think this world is yours? Eh?
And Rich Man, do you ever think this world is yours?
White Man, do you think this world is yours? Eh?
And you Black Man, do you ever think this world is yours?
Leaders, do you ever think this world is yours? Eh?
Presidents, oh yeah, do you ever think this world is yours?
If you're thinking so, my friends . . .
Better change your mind.
If you're thinking so, my friends . . .
Better change your mind.

No discussion of Nigerian and Ghanaian music in the 1970s would be complete without at least a brief discussion of Fela Anikulapo Kuti and the Afrobeat style that he helped pioneer. But attempting to briefly discuss the influence and life of Fela is no small trick. What can you say of a musician who helped create a now international music style and who used his public standing to fearlessly charge those in power in Nigeria (and elsewhere) with corruption. Who was repeatedly arrested and often tortured by a succession of Nigerian governments, who declared his home to be a sovereign nation (the Kalakuta Republic), and who at one point married all 27 of his backup vocalists? Who released over four dozen albums and now has a Broadway musical bearing his name?

Perhaps the best way to address Fela is to identify how he represents the creativity and alleged contradictions of the time and place in which he lived. Fela was born to a family that is generally identified as members of "Nigeria's Westernized Elite." His grandfather was a minister. His father another minister and teacher. His mother was a noted Nigerian nationalist and feminist. Like his two brothers, Fela was sent to London to study medicine, but switched fields to study jazz. While in London he formed two bands, first the Highlife Rakers, and then Koola Lobitos, which was an avant-jazz/Highlife fusion band that was partially inspired by artists such as Sun Ra and Thelonious Monk. Returning to West Africa in 1963, he performed with bands in Ghana and Nigeria, and also played in the backup band hired to play for Chubby Checker during his tour of Nigeria. A visit to the United States in 1969 opened up Fela's musical and political worlds, in no small part through the influence of Sandra Smith, who was a devotee of the Black Panthers.

Back in Nigeria, Fela renamed his band "Africa '70" (see Fig. 4.4) and continued his process of musical hybridization, blending Highlife and jazz with extra helpings of rock, funk, and soul. Fela also chose to

FIGURE 4.4   Fela and band (1975)

sing in "Broken" (short for "Broken English"), which is the creole mix of English words and Niger-Congo grammar that is spoken as a lingua-franca across much of West Africa. Indeed, it is a hybrid language, much as Afrobeat is hybrid music. It was a perfect match to make Fela's style both more distinctive and his songs accessible to a wide swath of populations across West Africa, Europe, and America.

As noted, Fela used the public platform of his music to criticize those in power. In "Zombie"(1977) he accused Nigerian soldiers of becoming unthinking monsters who acted in the service of a military dictatorship:

> Zombie no go go, unless you tell am to go
> Zombie no go stop, unless you tell am to stop
> Zombie no go turn, unless you tell am to turn
> Zombie no go think, unless you tell am to think

In "Coffin for Head of State" (1980) he told the story of carrying his mother's coffin to the seat of Nigeria's military government to demand that the current ruler, General Obasanjo, bury her (Fela asserted she had died from injuries sustained from being thrown from an upstairs window during an army raid on his home):

> Them steal all the money
> Them kill many students
> Them burn many houses
> Them burn my house, too
> Them kill my mama
>
> So I carry the coffin
> I waka waka waka
> Movement of the People
> Them waka waka waka
> Young African Pioneers
> Them waka waka waka
>
> We go Obalende
> We go Dodan barracks
> We reach them gate o
> We put dey coffin down
> Obasanjo dey der
> With de big fat stomach
> Yar'Adua dey there
> With de neck like ostrich
> We put de coffin down
> But them no want take am!
> Them no want to take am (x2)

Before his conflict with the government came to dominate his music, however, Fela often wrote songs to mock those he felt had turned their backs on what he considered African identity. In the song "Lady" he makes fun of "ladies" who aspire to status equal to or higher than men (and extolls the virtues of "African women" who do not do so):

> I want tell you about Lady
> She go say him equal to man
> She go say him get power like man
> She go say anything man do
> Himself he do
> I never tell you finish (x2)
> She go want take cigar before anybody
> She go want make you open door for am

She go want make man wash plate for am for kitchen
She won't salute man she go sit down for chair
She want sit down for table before anybody
She want take piece of meat before anybody
Call am for dance, she go dance Lady dance (×2)

African woman go dance she go dance the fire dance (×2)
She know him man na Master (×2)

And in such lyrics lies at least part the complexity that is Fela's music and the nature of African music during the twentieth century. Fela's music, like, jazz, soul, country, rock, Rai, Highlife, and a host of other styles, was very much the result of a multifaceted interaction that had gone on across Africa, across the Atlantic, and around the world for hundreds of years. Yet Fela considered it "African" and used it not only to demand justice from dictators, but also to mock others for their choice of dress and or to tell women their "proper place." To untangle and decode such meanings is no small task, and this complexity partially explains why the scholarly and popular literature about Fela has been growing so rapidly in recent years.

CONCLUSION: THE NATION, AFRICAN CULTURAL EPICUREANISM, AND GLOBALIZATION IN THE TWENTIETH CENTURY

The nature of African music in the latter twentieth century and its collision with constructions of what is and is not "African" do much to complicate our understanding of the continent and its inhabitants. Witness the following statement by the Cameroonian saxophone player Mann Dibango in 1978 in response to accusations that his music was "not African enough":

> What is Africa? I want these people to tell me. Because I play sax, does that mean I'm not playing African music? I'm proud to be African, but to me being African is not to be in jail with Africa. If you stay in your own circle you learn nothing.[20]

---

[20] Mann Dibango, interview by Chris Stapleton, "Manu's Afrovision," *Black Music*, May, 1978, p. 40, in Stapleton and May, 1987, p. 76.

In many ways, the content of this chapter reflects a tension that was crucial to the twentieth century: the collision between the early idea of the nation and the "death of distance." For much of the twentieth century, the construction of the nation was that of a community of people with a fixed identity—an identity that was rooted in shared culture, shared race, and shared values. Yet, because of the technological, political, and social changes that were propelling and accelerating the "death of distance," the people, ideas, and cultural elements that are the very building blocks of identity were becoming increasingly hard for those in power to control. How could you maintain the cultural and racial unity of a "nation" in the face of constantly shifting, multiplying, and merging populations and identities?" This was a challenge for every nation, and was all the more so for newly independent states faced with trying to build national identity almost from the ground up. Some states, such as seen in the case studies of Algeria and Tanzania, attempted to one degree or another to mold national identity by highlighting certain cultural elements and restricting others. But, as in the case studies of Ghana and Nigeria, some new nations apparently embraced the "cultural epicureanism" of their populations, and let the music flow free. Indeed, it is interesting that when the Nigerian government cracked down on Fela Kuti, they attacked the person and his ideas, but not the music itself. But in all the case studies, one outcome is clear. Populations across the African continent exerted their cultural sovereignty by selecting what they wanted from an ever-growing global musical and technological smorgasbord. Musical forms such as Rai and Afrobeat not only grew, adapted, and flourished, but they also spread to become part of the global cultural stew. In the process, African musicians and audiences created some of the world's most modern musical forms, and helped create a globalized culture, even before the term "globalization" had entered into our vocabulary.

REFERENCES AND FURTHER READINGS

Agawu, Kofi. *Representing African Music* (New York: Routledge, 2003).

Askew, Kelly. *Performing the Nation: Swahili Music and Cultural Politics in Tanzania* (Chicago: University of Chicago Press, 2002).

Collins, John. *West African Pop Roots* (Philadelphia: Temple University Press, 1992).

Feld, Stephen. *Jazz Cosmopolitanism in Accra: Five Musical Years in Ghana* (Durham, NC: Duke University Press, 2012).

Ivanska, Andrew. *Cultured States: Youth, Gender, and Modern Style in 1960's Dar Es Salaam* (Durham, NC: Duke University Press, 2011).

Marissa J. *Intonations: A Social History of Music and Nation in Luanda, Angola, from 1945 to Recent Times* (Athens, OH: Ohio University Press, 2008).

Nketia, J. H. Kwabena. *The Music of Africa* (New York: W.W. Norton, 1974).

Plageman, Nate. *Highlife Saturday Night: Popular Music and Social Change in Urban Ghana* (Burlington, IN: Indiana University Press, 2012).

Schade-Poulsen, Marc. *Men and Popular Music in Algeria: The Social Significance of Rai* (Austin, TX: University of Texas Press, 1999).

——"Which World: On the Diffusion of Algerian Rai to the West," in Karen Fog Olwig and Krirsten Hastrup, *Siting Culture: The Shifting Anthropological Object* (London: Routledge, 1997).

Stapleton, Chris and Chris May. *African All-Stars: The Pop Music of a Continent* (London: Quartet Books, 1987).

The Decolonization
of Distance: Ghana Enters
the Jet Age

There is an extensive literature on the era of decolonization and early independence in Africa. Most of it, not unlike the first three chapters of this text, has focused on political and economic issues. That is all well and good. When people think of sovereignty, they tend to think of political and economic freedoms first. Yet freedom of choice comes in many forms. The previous chapter, for example, looked at music. This chapter is going to look at a different kind of freedom—the freedom to move around. Indeed, the freedom to go where you want when you want is an expression of both economic and political sovereignty.

It is one of the ironies of colonial era that it both introduced the concept of motorized transport (whether by train, car, steamship, or airplane) to millions of Africans and at the same time erected a host of barriers to their ability to freely utilize such means of mobility. Some of these were barriers of cost, in that most colonized Africans simply could not afford a train ticket or even taxi fare. Further, colonial regulations in the form of security edicts, economic regulations, and colonial boundaries often placed extensive restrictions on the ability of Africans to move about as they saw fit. Such restrictions varied from one colony to the next and tended to be most extreme in colonies with significant European populations, such as Algeria, South Africa, or Kenya. In all colonies, however, the status that came with modern transport was a privilege jealously guarded by Europeans, be they colonial administrators, missionaries, or business people. Finally, the fact that Africans were subjects rather than citizens meant that only a tiny number could travel internationally—because only those individuals able to acquire passports could move about legally in a twentieth-century world divided by national boundaries. Thus, it was their command over distance that was one of the key means that allowed colonial powers to first establish and then maintain their economic and political hegemony.

And yet Europeans were unable to deny all aspects of motor transport to Africans. Economic factors required that some Africans traveled by rail or truck in order to move about the commodities and labor that fed colonial economies. Similarly, a tiny number of Africans gained the political influence and the wealth to purchase automobiles or travel internationally. Moreover, in the era after World War II, when African populations argued, agitated, and occasionally fought for their freedoms and African states moved toward independence, these restrictions on mobility began to be dismantled. This chapter focuses on Ghana during this heady time.

As we saw in Chapter 1, Ghana was a leader in the process of decolonization and became a center of Pan-African and global political activism. Fueled by a boom in cocoa prices, Ghanaians also enjoyed not only newfound political freedom, but also a standard of living that was the envy across much of the world. This newfound political freedom and economic wealth translated into a desire of Ghanaians to go places, both as individuals and as a nation. In this brief chapter, we use sources from the Ghanaian press to book a window seat on jet-age Ghana and get a view of how Ghanaians aspired to and understood the newfound potential to be not only independent of colonial restrictions on mobility, but also to have the world suddenly open up to them. In doing so, we address a number of questions and case studies. First, how did Ghanaians view motor transport as a signifier of social mobility? Second, how did the Ghanaian state view modern transport, particularly air travel, as a marker of modernity? Finally, what does the case study of two sets of very modern women, the winners of the annual Miss Ghana contest and the Ghana Airways "Air Girls" tell us about constructions of modern Ghanaian womanhood during this dynamic period of African history?

SOCIAL MOBILITY: TRANSPORT, RACE, CLASS, AND GENDER IN INDEPENDENCE-ERA GHANA

As already noted, during the heyday of colonialism in the early twentieth century, access to transport, especially that of motor cars and air travel, was largely limited to Europeans. This situation was a result of a complex mix of economic and political factors—many of which were rooted in the oppressive nature of colonialism itself. As a result, the marketing of automobiles and air travel in the colonies was aimed exclusively at Europeans. However, in the years after World War II, this situation began to change dramatically.

Ghanaian's movement toward political freedom was paralleled by another area of progress—the conquest of "white space" in print advertisements regarding motor transport. By the time of independence, advertisements regarding transport were no longer aimed exclusively at Europeans. Indeed, advertisers redesigned their ads to target Ghanaian buyers. For example, a Mobilgas ad from 1957 featured a Ghanaian "big man" dressed in a western suit and stating "Only the best for MY car!" as he gestured to his Rolls Royce.[1] Even those who could not afford a Rolls were featured as progressive customers. One ad clearly sought to make a distinction between Bedford brand busses and the "Mammy Wagons" which had served as public transport over the past few decades:

> Modern People go by Bedford Bus. When you travel in a Bedford Bus, you know what comfort really is! You relax in a roomy well-upholstered seat. You enjoy the most up-to-date standards of ease and cleanliness. And there's no scrambling with a Bedford Bus—you enter and leave in a dignified manner, by steps and a door. That's why modern people prefer to go by Bedford bus, it's the modern form of public transport.[2]

---

[1] *Daily Graphic*, July 9, 1957.
[2] *Daily Graphic*, December 10, 1960.

The imagery of the success represented by car ownership was even used to sell other products. Lennards Shoes used the motto "Walk to success in Lennards Shoes," and featured an arrow pointing to a businessman entering a car. An ad by Slumberland mattresses titled "Secret of his success" implied that being well rested was the secret to earning enough money to buy a car: "It's a big day for Tom. At last he can buy that car. The boss has just given him a better job with more money. He's a real success now."[3]

Of course, it is important to note that these ads did not exactly offer a clean break with the legacy of colonialism. They still sought to sell goods produced in the industrialized west (particularly Britain and the United States) to Africans, most of whose wealth came from producing and exporting unprocessed commodities. However, the shift portrayed in these advertisements is nonetheless significant in that they clearly portray that not only had Ghanaians broken the European monopoly on access to car ownership, but that European manufacturers and marketers took them seriously as a new and expanding market. Thus these advertisements reflected the reality that the newfound Ghanaian mobility was not only physical, but also social. Some Ghanaians could now cross barriers of race that had once been nearly impenetrable. Ghanaian independence and access to transportation, combined with newfound citizenship and civil liberties, were clearly resulting in a breakdown of colonial racial barriers.

In this vein, another significant development in what we might call the decolonization of distance came in 1959, when the first-ever Ghanaian team entered the Ghana Rally. Since the early twentieth century, Europeans living in the Gold Coast and elsewhere in Africa had enjoyed the privilege of motorsport competition, often in the form of timed "Motor Rallies." These events were opportunities to display not only European wealth and command over technology, but also their control over large chunks of land and the road system, since the roads were often closed to public and commercial traffic during the races. In the colonial Gold Coast, the largest of these events was the annual "Gold Coast Rally," which lasted several days and ran from Accra to Kumasi to Cape Coast and back to Accra. These events received considerable coverage in the *Daily Graphic* newspaper, often receiving multipage spreads of photos and featuring ads by auto manufacturers touting their products and congratulating the winners.

---

[3] *Daily Graphic*, October 14, 1958.

In the first year after independence, a story on the rally featured this comment:

> This form of sport makes for disciplined motoring. It is a pity that more motorists do not take part in it, especially the Africans. Let more of us show interest in it in the future.[4]

In 1959 Emmanuel Lomotey Annum did just that and received considerable press in the *Daily Graphic*, with the story featuring his photograph.[5] And well it should have, as motorsport was to colonial privilege much like baseball was to America. Annum was the Jackie Robinson of motorsports in Ghana. In 1961, Mr. A. Asamani-Kye became the first Ghanaian to win the event.

Mobility on the roads and access to motorsport, however, were not the only things that were becoming available to Ghanaians in the years following independence. Air transport, too, became increasingly accessible. This was not only a result of independence and the cocoa boom, but was also a side effect of the Cold War. Western European states, the United States, and the Soviet Union all sought to garner favor with newly independent Ghanaians via relatively open travel regulations and the frequent provision of subsidized travel for students, scholars, and government officials. Thus the period after independence saw a rapid increase in the number of Ghanaians traveling outside of the country. One BOAC (British Overseas Air Corporation) ad is particularly telling of this transition. This ad speaks to the pleasures of an extended layover in Europe when flying between Britain and Ghana and features a smiling European couple enjoying a meal in a Swiss restaurant. Just behind them, however, an artist has clearly penned in an African traveler, enjoying his own meal right along with them. Now, such images are always tricky to interpret. One meaning could be that BOAC was simply eager to make money from newly mobile Africans. Another interpretation would be to see this image as evidence of the successful African conquest of European mobility and privilege. Of course, the two interpretations need not be exclusive of one another.

Certainly international travel carried with it no small status in the context of Ghana in the 1950s and 1960s. Two advertisements

---

[4] Osenkafo, "Autocross is good sport," *Daily Graphic*, September 12, 1958.
[5] "The Great Car Rally," *Daily Graphic*, September 19, 1959.

The ZODIAC, ZEPHYR, and CONSUL models are perfect examples of combined design and engineering skill which produce a car to satisfy the most discriminating judge!

★ ★ ★ ★ ★
"Look the part in a 5 Star Ford"

W. BARTHOLOMEW
AND COMPANY LIMITED

Branches Throughout Ghana

FIGURE 5.1   "Ford Style," from the *Daily Graphic*

from the *Daily Graphic* are particularly representative of this reality. One, titled "Prominent people know the importance of FORD Style," (see Fig. 5.1) featured a student in graduation regalia disembarking from an airliner and walking to a new Ford automobile (complete with uniformed driver).[6] Here, the elision of air transport, foreign education, and automotive ownership is clearly portrayed. Another ad, this one for Grant's Whisky, portrayed a happy young Ghanaian in a swanky bar, sitting in front of a smiling European couple and bartender. The text of the ad read

> The man who has traveled widely knows that Grant's Stand Fast Whisky is one of the most famous in the world. He sees the smartest people ordering it in the best hotels and bars of New York, London and Paris. Wherever he goes in the world's big cities, he sees the tall triangular bottle of Grant's Stand Fast Whisky. It is the finest smoothest whisky. *When you order Grant's Stand Fast Whisky, you prove that you know good whisky.*

There are layers of meaning here that go well beyond just making Grant's Whisky seem sophisticated. Indeed, the desirability of Grant's

---

[6] *Daily Graphic*, April 16, 1958.

is clearly connected to the implication that it was a drink favored by a cosmopolitan class of people, white and black, who traveled freely from one major city to the next. Thus the reality that some Ghanaians could now travel in such a manner could be used to market Grant's Whisky to others who sought to get at least a taste of such cosmopolitanism.

Even those who could not afford air travel, however, were portrayed as a part of a mobile and modern Ghana. Even bicycle advertisements touted modernity and personal sovereignty. A Raleigh ad campaign in 1958–1959 was built around the slogan "Move with the times—on a cycle." One such ad featured a young nurse on a bike (complete with headlight) and read

> *Up to date women*—go by cycle. Every woman who leads a busy, active life needs a bicycle of her own. With a bicycle you're independent of public transport—and there are no fares to pay! Women all over the world ride bicycles, for business, visits to friends, shopping and pleasure trips. Cycling's the modern fashion for the modern woman. You too should own a bicycle.[7]

Another Raleigh ad featured a young man in a suit cycling past an airport with an airliner overhead:

> We go-ahead people want our own personal transport! Every man with up-to-date ideas wants to be free to travel when and where he pleases. A bicycle gives you this freedom! There's no expensive maintenance, no fares to pay, no tiresome waiting. Travel the modern way—by bicycle![8]

GHANA ENTERS THE JET AGE!

If motor transport had been an area of colonial privilege, air travel was even more so, as it demanded even greater degrees of wealth and sovereignty than its ground-bound cousin. Further, the display of the command of technology that came with air transport was part and parcel of the display of technological prowess and power that Michal Adas has argued served to both facilitate and justify ongoing colonial domination. Perhaps nothing better illustrates this

---

[7] *Daily Graphic*, April 2, 1958.
[8] *Daily Graphic*, December 16, 1959.

early twentieth-century reality than the iconic advertisements used by *Air Afrique*, the French colonial-era air service in Africa. One such ad features a colonial agent gazing down from his aircraft window at the ground beneath him, while holding a map of Africa in his hand. The implication is clear that he is in command of the continent, which is literally beneath him. Quite in contrast, another series of *Air Afrique* ads featured Africans gazing up in amazement as the *Air Afrique* plane soared overhead, out of reach and even perhaps beyond comprehension.

It is clear that the newly independent government of Ghana sought to erase the technology gap that served to make Africa accessible to Europeans but Europe out of reach to Africans. One article in a special *Daily Graphic* supplement on travel was titled "Let US Go Abroad, Let THEM Come Here" (original emphasis). At the same time, Nkrumah's government was also displaying its own legitimacy by appropriating the symbols of colonial rule and "Ghana-izing" them. To this end, the story of the creation and expansion of Ghana Airways was often front-page news during the early years after independence. Indeed, the role of print media such as newspapers in the creation of national identities has been identified by a number of scholars, not the least of whom is Benedict Anderson.[9]

Announcements regarding the government's plans to develop a national air carrier began in April of 1958, less than a year after independence. The first of these stories was titled "Whispering Giants to Fly on W. A. Routes" and announced the plans to purchase new planes to fly to and from Europe as well as to expand domestic service within Ghana.[10] In June a front-page story showed the minster for transportation sitting in the pilot's seat of an aircraft being tested for possible purchase.[11] Another story in the same issue announced that the post office would issue stamps to commemorate the launching of a national airline. Another front-page story followed on July 5, with a banner headline announcing "Air Ghana Pact Signed" and featured a photo of President Nkrumah and other CPP officials signing an agreement with BOAC to establish Ghana Airways. The story also announced that the government was allocating £400,000 to found the company.

---

[9] Heck . . . you can't swing a dead cat without hitting an homage to Anderson in the literature on early independence.

[10] "Whispering Giants to Fly on W.A. Routes," *Daily Graphic*, April 21, 1958, p. 16.

[11] "Ghana Tests Plane," *Daily Graphic*, June 27, 1958.

Wasting no time, another front-page story titled "Air Ghana's First Trip" was featured on July 16 and included a picture of President Nkrumah disembarking from the newly painted Ghana Airways airplane (another story in the same issue of the paper showed the plane being repainted in the colors of the Ghanaian flag) after its first demonstration flight.[12] All of these elements, including the painting of the plane, the flight, the presence of Nkrumah, and the front-page story, were something of "performances" of both nationhood and modernization. The day was declared "Ghana Airline Day," and the entire spectacle was a display of Ghana's rapid progress now that the brakes of colonialism had been taken off. A story on the following day announced "Many queue to buy Ghana Airways Stamps."[13]

Over the next several years, stories and advertisements featuring Ghana Airways continuously reminded the Ghanaian public that progress was being made. In August of 1958, for example, a two-page center spread in the *Daily Graphic* announced "Ghana is entering the Jet Age." Following the subheading of "Modern Giants of the Skies," a story reinforced that idea that Ghana's acquisition of modern technology was decolonizing distance and changing history (see Fig. 5.2):

> These graceful silver and blue giants of the sky—which will be flying in the Livery of GHANA AIRWAYS—racing with smooth power above the palm trees, the sparkling beaches, and the warm rich red earth, will bring West Africa within even shorter traveling time of Europe. With the introduction of these jet planes a new page will be written in the history of civil aviation in West Africa.[14]

As Ghana Airways acquired new planes in the coming years, each acquisition was chronicled in detail, featuring photographs of the planes and showing the "ceremony" of them being painted in Ghanaian colors—once again a clear display that the technology they represented was now "Ghanaian." When Ghana Airways acquired its first jet passenger craft in the form of the British-made Vickers VC-10, the aircraft's popular acclaim was evident by the aircraft's being featured on

---

[12] "Air Ghana's First Trip" and "Painting Ghana Colours on Plane," *Daily Graphic*, July 16, 1958, front page and p. 9.

[13] "Many queue to buy Ghana Airways Stamps," *Daily Graphic*, July 17, 1958.

[14] "Ghana is entering the Jet Age," *Daily Graphic*, August 16, 1958. As a technical note, the Britannia aircraft purchased by Ghana Airways were not strictly "jet" aircraft. They were turboprop planes, which used jetlike turbines to power the propellers that powered them in flight.

112   *Sovereignty and Struggle*

FIGURE 5.2   "Ghana is Entering the Jet Age," from the *Daily Graphic*

cloth sold for women's wrappers. One truck driver humorously decorated his truck with the moniker "Vickers VC 9 & 3/4."[15]

The aircraft also served to help display Ghana as an up-and coming nation on the regional and global stage as well. Nkrumah, for example, utilized Ghana Airways planes for official state visits to Nigeria (with which Ghana had something of a rivalry for regional influence) and to close allies such as Nasser's Egypt.[16] The establishment of regular routes to Cairo and Beirut in 1961 highlighted Ghana's links not only across Africa and to Europe, but to other leading states in the "developing world" as well. Indeed, the close air ties to Cairo helped to cement Nkrumah's close ties to Nasser in the building of Pan-Africanism. Ghana Airways was also touted by Nkrumah as a tool for Pan-Africanism. As one article stated ". . . it was the wish of Osagyefo that Ghana Airways

---

15 Kojo Gyinaya Kyei and Hannah Schreckenbach, *No Time To Die* (Private Publication: Ghana, 1975), p. 69.

16 A front page story from January 27th, 1959, for example, showed Nkrumah arriving in Nigeria for a state visit. The photograph was carefully framed so as to show that Nkrumah was disembarking from a Ghana Airways plane.

should play a major role in African Unity by linking the independent African states."[17] The fact that it was Ghana Airways that was helping to break down colonial divisions could only serve to strengthen Ghana's image as a driving force behind African unity.

The nature of Ghana Airway's fleet also reflected Ghana's shifting political position vis-à-vis the Cold War. The initial purchase of British aircraft reflected the countries continuing ties to its former colonial ruler. However, in November of 1960, the country acquired the first three of six Ilyushin turboprop aircraft from the Soviet Union. Such a purchase was loaded with international symbolism. To some it showed that Ghana was carefully balancing itself as a nonaligned state. To others, particularly in the US government, it was a dangerous sign that Ghana was slipping toward becoming a Soviet client. The fact that the newspaper story celebrating the maiden flight of one of the planes featured a photo of Nkrumah enjoying a champagne toast with the Russian ambassador aboard the plane was no doubt a source of Western diplomatic angst and Soviet hopes. Shortly afterward, however, the Ghanaians placed an order for three US-made Boeing 707s.

GHANA AND GLOBAL GLAMOUR

As we have seen in previous chapters, Africa was not the only part of the world undergoing a social and political transformation in the years following World War II. In particular, women's roles in many countries were changing dramatically as many women pushed for new educational, social, and professional roles. The sexual revolution, too, began to transform both how society viewed women and how women viewed themselves.

In this tumultuous time two new symbols of modern womanhood began to emerge around the world: the glamorous stewardess and the national beauty queen. In the 1950s, as air travel around the world expanded and grew safer and faster, the role of flight attendants shifted away from nursing and safety and more toward making flying a luxurious experience. Kathleen M. Barry has characterized flight attendants during the period as the "Glamour Girls of the Air."[18] Interestingly, although male pilots enjoyed a certain amount of cachet, it was the

---

[17] "Ghana Airways Lost £484,271," *Daily Graphic,* May 30, 1963.
[18] Barry, 2007, pp. 36–59.

stewardesses who captured much of the public imagination of the new era. From pulp fiction to cover stories in magazines such as *Life*, as well as in movies and on television, stewardesses became icons of modernity during the period.[19]

Just as the 1950s saw a surge in air travel, the rapid expansion of television also helped give rise to the institution of the Beauty Pageant. Long inhabiting the extremes of the risqué or the local and quaint, television moved beauty contests to the mainstream, not only on the national, but also on the global level. In the United States and Britain, the Miss USA and Miss World competitions, respectively, were the most highly viewed programs offered annually during the early 1960s. Notably, the incorporation of public-speaking elements in the competitions, the provision of scholarships to the winners, and the added element of national competition at the Miss World level helped to add a certain level of respectability to these events.

Similarly, as Ghana was taking part in the jet age by launching Ghana Airways, Ghana was representing modern femininity with the airline's stewardesses, known as the "Air Girls," and by taking part in the Miss World Beauty Pageant. Much as in the case of Ghana Airways, the selection of the Air Girls and Miss Ghana and their exploits were often front-page news, highlighting not only their importance to the construction of Ghanaian notions of modernity, but also Ghana's participation in the global craze for stewardesses and beauty queens that was taking place at the time.

THEY'LL MAKE THE AIR GHANAIAN!

Images of stewardesses began to appear in the Ghanaian press even before the launch of Ghana Airways. In March of 1958, the West African Airways Corporation (WAAC, a regional airline run by BOAC) ran a large ad with the banner "YOU too can FLY as an Air Stewardess with West African Airways Corporation" and featuring an image of a young African woman pointing upward—a none-too-subtle reference to personal as well as technological progress. The body of the ad stated

> Unique opportunities to fly with West African Airways Corporation as Air Stewardesses are offered to girls who possess the necessary qualifications.

---

[19] See, for example, Omelia and Waldock, 2006, and Stein, 2006.

Successful candidates may eventually fly on West African Airways Corporation's International services between West Africa and the United Kingdom or on the West Coast or Internal services, after successful completion of advanced training in West Africa.[20]

As proof that being selected for and completing such training was deemed newsworthy, when Johanna Ashirifie, the first Ghanaian to complete the WAAC course returned from training in Lagos, Nigeria, she was featured in a photo expose in the *Daily Times*. The story noted that she would first serve on West African flights, but would soon move to serve on the "Rome, Tripoli, and London routes."[21] She was featured again roughly one year later, in a story celebrating the first flight of a Bristol Britannia operated by BOAC to Ghana. The article featured a photo of Ms. Ashirifie (along with a European stewardess) greeting the British governor-general after landing at the airport.[22]

Media attention to Ghanaian stewardesses began to dramatically increase as Ghana Airways was established (see Fig. 5.3). In July of 1959, a front-page story announced "Three Air Girls to Study in Britain." This story, interestingly, was the first appearance of the term "Air Girls," a moniker that was to remain in use for the duration of the era. The story featured photos of each of the three hostesses being sent to train in London.[23] The role of the Air Girls (and Ghanaian Airways) in representing Ghana internationally was also highlighted in a story in November of 1959 that reported that members of the Ghanaian parliament had called for the hostesses to wear uniforms featuring Kente Cloth and to serve Ghanaian food on international flights.[24]

The coverage of the Air Girls reached a new level when a group of ten hostesses was sent to London for training in March of 1960. This story featured a large front-page headline announcing "The first picture of our new AIR GIRLS." Under the banner, italicized text described the image:

A beauty parade? Not exactly . . . it's a line-up of ten smiling girls waiting at Accra airport to board a plane for the United Kingdom to train as stewardesses for service with Ghana Airways.

---

[20] *Daily Graphic*, March 20, 1958, p. 11.
[21] "She is first Ghanaian air hostess," *Daily Graphic*, April 1, 1958.
[22] "Ghana Greets the Britannia – The Whispering Giant Arrives. Champagne at 15,000 Feet," *Daily Graphic*, April 6, 1959, pp. 6–7.
[23] "Three Air Girls to Study in Britain," *Daily Graphic*, July 21, 1959, p. 1.
[24] "Air Girls may wear kente on special flights," *Daily Graphic*, November 21, 1959, p. 3.

FIGURE 5.3   "On Top of the World," from the *Daily Graphic*

FIGURE 5.4   "Make the Air Ghanaian," from the *Daily Graphic*

Interestingly, the photo of the Air Girls also featured four men, two of them Ghana Airways directors and two of them from the Ghanaian Ministry of Transport—an association that only served to reinforce that the Air Girls were not just employees of Ghana Airways, but were also partners in the government campaign to construct a modern and cosmopolitan image of Ghana.[25]

The coverage of this group of air girls did not end with their leaving Ghana either. On this trip they were accompanied by a *Daily Graphic* reporter. A short time later, the newspaper featured a two-page center-spread story on the hostesses' training under the banner headline "They'll make the Air Ghanaian!" (see Fig. 5.4) The story

---

[25] "The First Picture of our new AIR GIRLS," *Daily Graphic*, March 11, 1960, p. 1.

featured such elements of the Air Girl's training as learning to exercise so as to maintain a "healthy figure" and how to properly apply makeup.[26] The fact that the more professional aspects of the hostesses' training were not deemed newsworthy says much about the notions of women's professional characteristics during the period. As noted earlier, such an emphasis on physical attributes was typical not only of Ghanaian coverage of the Air Girls but was also characterized by much of the popular press focusing on stewardesses around the world.

Indeed, an article from January 6, 1960, titled "Do You want to become an Air Girl? Here is how to find out your fitness for the job," enumerated the characteristics of a successful candidate in the form of a series of questions that speaks volumes about the nature of women's work at the time. The fact that the questions were clearly cribbed from an American or European manual also highlights that the Air Girls were contesting racialized European space—in this case a professional space dominated by "natural blonds":

1. Are your looks outstanding?
3. Can you mix a dry martini or a Tom Collins?
9. Are you a natural blond?
10. Are you in love? (If so, you were of "no use to the company.")
11. Can you converse easily with strange men?
17. Can you wear a thin, well-cut uniform and make it look neat without bulging in the wrong places?
23. Do these questions embarrass you?

MISS GHANA AT THE WHEEL

If the Air Girls had any competition for the nonexistent title of "Official Modern Ghanaian Woman," it was Miss Ghana. Beginning in 1959, the very year that the Miss World competition was televised by the BBC (British Broadcasting Corporation), Ghana selected its first "Miss Ghana" and sent her to compete in the international competition in London. Notably, a newspaper story stated that the contest was held in "connection with Ghana's second independence anniversary."[27] A rather unique way to commemorate national sovereignty, indeed.

---

[26] "They'll Make the Air Ghanaian," *Daily Graphic*, March 23, 1960, pp. 8–9.
[27] "Miss Ghana at the Wheel," *Daily Graphic*, June 9, 1959, p. 3.

Unlike the Air Girls, who were selected to meet what might be loosely considered European or American standards of beauty, the first winner of the Miss Ghana contest, Mrs. Elizabeth Hayford, clearly played by a more Ghanaian set of rules. For example, the winner of the first "Miss Ghana" pageant was a Mrs. And, quite unlike the vast majority of national beauty queens, Mrs. Elizabeth Hayford was not only married, but was a mother as well.

In many ways, Mrs. Hayford represented a more conservative version of Ghanaian womanhood, both at home and abroad. For example, she almost always appeared wearing "traditional" garb in the form of a wrapper, though it was often offset by a more European-style tailored blouse. Yet, Miss Ghana was also a representative of the new Ghanaian mobility that was so celebrated in the pages of the *Daily Graphic*. In particular, the grand prize for the pageant was a trip to London to compete in the televised Miss World contest. While there, she was featured in a number of stories and ads for the United Africa Company (the sponsors of the Miss Ghana Contest). One ad in particular highlighted her independence and cosmopolitanism. This one was titled "MISS GHANA toured London in a VAUXHALL Victor" and featured a photo of Miss Ghana posed confidently with the car in Trafalgar Square (Figure 5.5) and apparently describing her experience:

I saw all the wonderful sights of London through the big wide windows of the Vauxhall Victor, they give you a perfect view all round! And what a comfortable car the Victor is—the seats are so soft and the springing is so good that fast driving seems like flying! But most of all I like the Victors lovely colours, inside and out, and its big modern look.[28]

Notably, Miss Ghana was also associated with motoring in Ghana. For example, she presented the trophies to the 1959 winners of the Ghana Motor Rally. She also had a brief experience with the Air Girls. On July 14, 1959, a front-page story pictured Mrs. Hayford being trained as a "ground stewardess" by one of the Air Girls. The story stated that Mrs. Hayford was to be trained as an air hostess at a later date, though it appears that this never came to pass.[29] Nonetheless, the story does point up the fact that there was no small overlap in the representation of modernity in Ghana (as elsewhere) during this

---

[28] *Daily Graphic*, August 29, 1959.
[29] "Women in the News: Learning to be a hostess," *Daily Graphic*, July 14, 1959, p. 1.

MISS GHANA toured London

in a **VAUXHALL** Victor

" I saw all the wonderful sights of London through the big wide windows of the Vauxhall Victor, they give you a perfect view all round! And what a comfortable car the Victor is — the seats are so soft and the springing is so good that fast driving seems like flying! But most of all I like the Victor's lovely colours, inside and out, and its big modern look."

Miss Ghana is right! The Vauxhall Victor has all the style and all the comfort — plus amazing economy! Prove this for yourself — let us arrange a demonstration drive free of all cost and obligation.

960 GMY

VAUXHALL SALES AND SERVICE FROM **U.A.C. MOTORS**

AGGRA ▲ KUMASI ▲ TAKORADI

FIGURE 5.5   "Ms. Ghana," from the *Daily Graphic*

period. Beauty, aircraft, cars, and government all seemed to go together. Beauty pageant winners were often shown traveling by air and often in connection with stewardesses or government officials. For example, the winner of the *Mirror Newspaper* beauty contest, Florence Kotei, won a flight to Lagos, Nigeria, in 1959, where she dined with the Ghanaian high commissioner.[30] Even Nigerian beauty queens were worthy of Ghanaian coverage. In September of 1959, the *Daily Graphic* featured a front-page story of Miss Nigeria displaying Nigerian crafts to two Pan-American stewardesses at the New York International Airport.[31] Perhaps what is most interesting is just how complex these images and stories are. Not unlike the history of early African independence, there is no simple message.

CONCLUSION: INDEPENDENCE, MODERNITY, AND THE CRISES OF EXPECTATIONS

The early years of Ghanaian independence were heady times, defined by optimism and exuberance. Sadly, this period was short lived. Indeed, Ghana Airway's fortunes were to serve as something of a barometer for the entire Ghanaian economy. The airline's rapid growth at first mirrored the optimism of Ghana after independence. By 1963, Ghana Airways could boast two Herons, four Dakotas, two Britannias, and six Ilyushins. In 1962–1963 they carrier transported nearly 25,000 domestic passengers and nearly 13,000 on routes to Europe. And yet this apparent success of Ghana Airways came at a huge operational cost. Indeed, the airline failed to earn a profit in 1960–1961, posting a loss of some £33,000. By 1962–1963 this loss had grown to £484,271, a staggering sum at the time. Worse, the collapse in global cocoa prices around this same time meant that Ghana went from having a net trade surplus to a significant trade deficit—a deficit that meant that the country could ill afford not only new aircraft, but also the symbols of mobility and cosmopolitanism that had so been celebrated in the early years of independence. Orders for a number of aircraft, including the Boeings and additional VC-10s were canceled by the Ghanaian government. For Ghanaian citizens, even those living in the country's cosmopolitan cities and working in government and

---

[30] "Queen on Her First Flight," *Daily Graphic*, November 4, 1959, p. 1.
[31] "It's all Nigerian Made!," *Daily Graphic*, September 10, 1959, p. 1.

business, goods such as cars, new beds, and Grant's Stand Fast Whisky became increasingly difficult to afford.

The literature on Africa over the era since World War II has made much of the apparent failure of African states to deliver on the promises and hopes that independence brought to the continent. The most popular term for this phenomenon is "the crises of expectations." This is the idea that Africans' expectations were simply unrealistic and doomed to failure. The failure of countries such as Ghana to speedily deliver political stability, economic progress, and improved quality of life in general would seem, at first glance, to bear this perspective out. The anthropologist James Ferguson has gone so far as to declare that "The modernization narrative was always a myth, an illusion, often even a lie." However, perhaps there is another, rather more positive, way to look at the example of Ghana and that of other African states during the first decades since independence. The exuberance was real—because the hope was real. The hope was not so much based on a myth as it was on an all too brief reality. And Africans were not alone in envisioning a bright future. Politicians, activists, and businesspeople around the world also imagined that the policies of independence would lead to a prosperous and "modern" Africa. Certainly the US company Kaiser Aluminum didn't invest millions in Ghana in expectation that the venture would fail in the near term. Raleigh didn't advertise their bicycles to "modern women" in Africa because they thought the idea was silly.

Indeed, the fact is that getting (or even maintaining) sovereignty during the Cold War was a hard row to hoe, pretty much everywhere. Given such a setting it is worth noting that Africans nonetheless created a new, "modern," and often intensely cosmopolitan Africa, despite the challenges and disappointments of the early independence era. Certainly there was corruption and all too often conflict. But those things have been staples of human existence for millennia, and Africa by no means cornered the market on such misfortunes. This, too, is one of the advantages of looking at Africa in global context. More so, it is important to keep in mind that there were significant achievements even in the face of extreme hardship and a complicated global context. The ongoing struggle and eventual achievement of liberation in Southern Africa is one. Africa's continued process of cultural exchange and creation, as evidenced by the continent's vibrant arts and music, is another. The fact that so many Africans, even in the worst of times, went on about their lives despite daily hardships that would reduce many in ostensibly "more successful" countries to panic and despair highlights the power of Africans to persevere even in the face of dashed hopes.

Finally, it is important to note that every low point is, after all, a turning point. Africa in the 1980s and early 1990s to some may have seemed a case study in human failures. Few who took the time to categorize the continent's failures would have forecast that in 2014 the continent would be home to some of the world's fastest growing economies and that *The Economist* magazine, which once characterized Africa as "The Hopeless Continent," would be sponsoring workshops for eager investors, seeking, once again, to profit from an apparent African boom.

REFERENCES AND FURTHER READINGS

Adas, Michael. *Machines as the Measure of Men: Science, Technology, and Ideologies of Western Dominance* (Ithaca, NY: Cornell University Press, 1990).

Barber, Karin. *Readings in African Popular Culture* (Bloomington, IN: Indiana University Press, 1997).

Barry, Kathleen M. *Femininity in Flight: A History of Flight Attendants* (Durham, NC: Duke University Press, 2007).

Benedict, Anderson. *Imagined Communities: Reflections on the Origin and Spread of Nationalism* (New York: Verso, 2006).

Ferguson, James. *Expectations of Modernity: Myths and Meanings of Urban Life on the Zambian Copperbelt* (Oakland, CA: University of California Press, 1999).

Hart, Jennifer. *"Suffer to Gain": Citizenship, Accumulation, and Motor Transportation in Late-Colonial and Postcolonial Ghana.* (PhD Dissertation, Indiana University, 2011).

Kyei, Kojo Gyinaye and Hannah Schreckenbach. *No Time To Die* (Accra, Ghana: Safeway Printing Works, 1999).

Omelia, Johanna and Michael Waldock. *Come Fly with Us! A Global History of the Airline Hostess* (Singapore: Collectors Press, 2006).

Stein, Elissa. *Stewardess: Come Fly with Me!* (San Francisco, CA: Chronicle Books, 2006).

Walker, Timothy and Scott Henderson. *Silent, Swift, Superb: Story of the Vickers VC10* (Newcastle Upon Tyne, UK: Scoval Publishing, 1998).

CREDITS

INDEX